A BLOODY
GOOD WINNER

A BLOODY GOOD WINNER

Life as a Professional Gambler

Dave Nevison
with David Ashforth

A **RACING POST** COMPANY

Published in 2007 by Highdown
an imprint of Raceform Ltd
Compton, Newbury, Berkshire, RG20 6NL

A catalogue record for this book is available from the British Library.

ISBN 978-1-905156-35-1

Designed by Adrian Morrish

Printed and bound in Great Britain by William Clowes Ltd, Beccles, Suffolk

CONTENTS

INTRODUCTION

When I've won £10,000, which I did yesterday, I like to celebrate. I don't want to drive home and write it in a ledger, then sit and gloat, like some miser in a long dark coat in a Charles Dickens novel. If I've had a big win I drink, I dance, sometimes I even sing. I've been known to stand on a table. I've been known to fall off. Not everyone approves of this. There is probably tut-tutting, shaking of heads and comment on the fact that I am 45 and should know better. But the way I look at it, most days aren't winning days and life is not always going well, so when it is, I make the most of it, while I can. I'm not a bad loser but I'm a bloody good winner, and if a big ship comes in I like people to know about it. I don't keep quiet, smile contentedly to myself and stroll down from the grandstand unnoticed. I shout, loudly.

Of course, I need the money, but I'm also addicted to the thrill of getting it right. If I do, it makes me happy, and when I'm happy, I celebrate. If I've backed a long-priced winner and the grandstand goes silent, I make the loudest noise possible because there are a lot of idiot punters on the racecourse who always yell when the favourite goes in. When I've backed a winner that they just could not find, I want to let them know that I was on it, because I'm better at punting than they are. I've got a big ego.

So, I'm a very good celebrator, and I'm gregarious. I like to have a good time with my friends. Yesterday evening we started off with a couple of bottles of Montrachet and Gevrey-Chambertin. I don't know much about wine, but those ones taste wonderful, and when I've had a particularly good day, that's what I get.

I expect you want to know how I won the £10,000. I'll tell you. (And then I'll tell you how I've made a living, a good living, the only kind I'm interested in, working as a professional gambler. Even better, I'll tell you the truth. It might help you, it might not. You just can't help most gamblers. You may be one of them.) I won it by having £500 at 20-1 on a horse called Rising Cross in the Park Hill Stakes at York on 8 September 2006. It's a very good win, but I've won £10,000 a lot of times.

Rising Cross is a horse I know particularly well, because I used to own part of her. With some newcomers to racehorse ownership I formed the Heading for the Rocks Partnership and bought Rising Cross for €20,000. That's very little for a racehorse, but then she is a little racehorse. Little body, but big heart: no effort too great to make, no gap too small to battle through – that precious creature, a racehorse who tries as hard as she can. By September 2006 we no longer owned her, having sold her to Gary Tanaka for £325,000 after she finished second in the Epsom Oaks. I backed her at York because I thought 20-1 was too long a price; I thought she had a better chance than that. That is always why I back a horse, because I think the horse has a better chance of winning than the odds available suggest. I thought 12-1 was a more accurate reflection of her chance of winning the race. Of course, she was still much more likely to lose than to win. In gambling there are always a lot more defeats than victories. But that doesn't matter as long as the victories more than make up for the defeats. You can lose a lot of battles and still win the war, as long as you haven't already committed suicide.

I don't know how Gary Tanaka celebrated – he was under house arrest in New York at the time on fraud charges – but, unusually for me, I celebrated quietly. I was in bed by one a.m. and up at five for another big day, St Leger day. Today.

The big racedays are my big betting days.

At the moment, they are busy knocking down Doncaster racecourse and building another one, so the St Leger is being held at York. I'm in my city-centre hotel room surrounded by a collection of ratings: John Whitley's, Timeform's, Raceform Interactive's. I don't do my own ratings. I used to, but I got bored with it. My strength lies in interpreting other people's figures.

Early breakfast. Fruit, two natural yogurts, coffee. I eat quite healthily. On the other hand, I eat quite a lot.

At 7.30 a.m. I make my first telephone call of the day, to my business partner, Mark Smith. We are in this together. Ten minutes later I'm on the phone to Neal Wilkins, who represents bookmaker Victor Chandler. On Saturdays, the bookmakers price the big races up early, because they don't want to miss out on all the banknotes that are waving about looking for a home. If they aren't answering the phone, a rival bookmaker will be. Neal's in bed, so I phone the organ grinder in Gibraltar. I want £5,000 to £900 on Hogmaneigh in the Portland Handicap, the first race of the day and a big betting sprint handicap, with nineteen runners. It's the sort of race a lot of punters don't like. Not me. I like races like that, big handicaps, with sixteen or more runners, the ones that pay out on the fourth place in each-way bets. Mathematically, punters often have an edge in those races.

Victor Chandler is a client-based bookmaker. His team know their clients inside out. If you've established your credentials as a mug punter, they will take a bet they wouldn't take from a shark. Now and again, the mug may want £1,000 on a horse that Victor doesn't really want to lay, but he wants to keep the mug happy. He knows that in the long run the mug's money is going only one way – Victor's way. The shark is different. Victor doesn't want to keep him happy. He wishes the shark would go away, because sharks have a horrible habit of biting. Victor hasn't become rich by being bitten, but he may put up with a small nip. So I have a nibble here, and a nibble there, trying to seem like a fairly harmless shark. The £900 isn't my last word on Hogmaneigh, but it's probably the biggest word Victor Chandler will listen to.

'Yes, that's all right.'

Why Hogmaneigh? Because in my book he's an 11-4 chance, yet he's 11-2 with three bookmakers: Victor Chandler, BetDirect and Betfred. I don't try the last two because, in my experience, it is difficult to get on. Getting on can be harder work than deciding what to back. If Hogmaneigh wins, Chandler hasn't necessarily been a mug because he's obtained a professional's opinion for not very much money. Taking my bet could cost him £5,000, but if he cuts Hogmaneigh's price because I've backed it, it could save him much more than that. On the other hand, he'll almost certainly cut the price anyway, because at 11-2 he's offering better odds than most other bookmakers, so all the money for Hogmaneigh will be flying his way.

I've already backed Sixties Icon for the St Leger, ante-post. I've had £2,000 at 5-1 and £3,000 at 7-2. That's over £20,000 profit if he wins. Earlier this week I laid the same horse for £1,000 on Betfair at 11-10, and I've just laid another £1,000 at 13-8. In other words, I backed him to lose at much shorter prices than I've backed him to win. I'm tempted to lay the lot and guarantee myself a profit. It's a question of whether I've got the bottle to hold on.

It's often like this. Five days before a race I think a horse I've backed is an absolute certainty, then I start to have doubts. On Monday, I thought Sixties Icon was a certainty.

He's the only really progressive horse over the St Leger trip, but now he's a very short price and Jeremy Noseda, his trainer, has sent out twenty losers in a row. You are bound to wonder, but I hang on.

Breakfast over, I drive to York racecourse, one of my favourites. It's a beautiful course, and this early in the morning it's crisp and quiet. The press room is deserted, which is what I want it to be. There's more work to be done. With Raceform Interactive on the screen, I go through each race and price up each horse. Then I compare my prices with the prices on offer.

And I find a perfect horse to take on. Wasseema has won her last three races impressively, is trained by champion trainer Sir Michael Stoute, and is generally 9-2 second favourite for the Park Stakes. She's 9-2 with the bookmakers, but she's 14-1 with me. Why?

When horses win as easily as Wasseema won at Ascot, by seven lengths, it usually says more about the beaten horses and the way the race panned out than it does about the winner. All three of her wins have been in fillies races, all over a mile, and in each of them she bossed the field. Today is different. Wasseema will be racing against Group 1 horses like Iffraaj and Speciosa, over seven furlongs, and she won't get an easy lead, because Speciosa and Welsh Emperor will be up there with her. She comes out well in the Whitley and Timeform ratings, but I don't believe it. Unless she's the champion filly of the year, she can't win. I don't lay horses much – I have a phenomenal record of laying winners – but I'll be laying Wasseema.

More phone calls to Mark. His main job is to put the bets on. If he can't get them on, I'll get others to put them on for me. I have a hardcore of friends who have no connection with racing and will be friends for life, and others who are friends purely for putting bets on. It's ruthless, I suppose, and it often ends in tears, but never in animosity. People put bets on for me, and in return they get to know what I am backing. At the end of it all, they are often worse off than they were before, because most of them are bad punters, losing punters, and if they make money from backing what I am backing it just gives them more funds to lose with. Why don't they just back the horses I give them? I don't know why. You tell me. That's just the way they are, and sometimes it causes problems. Sometimes they don't give me my winnings, they can't give me my winnings, at least not for a while, because they've lost them. So I have to find someone else to put bets on for me. I am constantly looking for new putters-on.

What I should really do is tell them the story of Gary Wiltshire, the six grand and the nostrils, as an encouragement. Wiltshire is a racecourse bookmaker, a big man, larger than other men, larger than life, best known for having lost an enormous sum of money, one with lots of noughts on the end, when Frankie Dettori rode all seven winners at Ascot on 28 September 1996 – a red-letter day for Frankie but a black armband day for Wiltshire. I owed Gary £6,000. At a Monday meeting at Wolverhampton I told him I'd give him his money on the Wednesday, but as things turned out I didn't go to Wolverhampton that day. When I saw him on the Friday, with most of the money, he told me that a couple of days ago he'd been to a greyhound meeting. 'I only went because this guy owed me a fortune,' he explained. 'He owed me seventy grand and said he was going to turn up with some of it, and when he turned up, you know what, he'd only brought a grand with him. You know what I did?'

'No,' I replied.

'I stuck my fingers so far up his nostrils that I lifted him a foot off the ground.'

A picture formed in my mind. It wasn't a very attractive one.

'Anyway,' Wiltshire continued, 'he paid me yesterday.'

'Yes, I suppose he would,' I said.

When I left Wolverhampton, Gary had his six grand.

8.50 a.m. I ring Mark to go through the Portland Handicap with him. Apart from Hogmaneigh, I want to back three others, each-way: Pivotal's Princess, Woodcote and Connect. The trouble is, Pivotal's Princess and Connect are Pricewise's bets of the day. Pricewise is the *Racing Post*'s lead tipster, with a huge following. The early-morning prices for his selections will soon be galloping over the horizon. I also want to lay Lafi, The Jobber and Fantasy Believer. If they fight out the finish, it'll be a disaster, about as costly as the Iraq war, but with fewer deaths. Just mine.

Hogmaneigh's trainer is rumoured to be thinking of pulling Hogmaneigh out because of the fast ground. I think that's bollocks. Maybe someone's started the rumour deliberately, to put punters off and stop the price shrinking. I'm more worried about the track, the draw, and Hogmaneigh's racing style. He is a hold-up horse, and at York, races tend to be won by horses racing up with the pace. Most of the pace is likely to be on the stand side, but Hogmaneigh is drawn on the other side. On the other hand, he may just be different class. If it weren't for those doubts, I'd be going in more heavily.

At ten o'clock I phone Mark and tell him we've got to be against Wasseema every way we can. In the same race, we have £200 each-way on Somnus, at 25-1. I didn't expect to be backing him but in my book I'm backing a 12-1 shot at 25-1, which is what I always want to do.

The brass band strikes up. Sometimes it sounds jolly, sometimes like a funeral service. How it sounds depends on how the bets go. Oompah, oompah.

The press are drifting in. Alastair Down, bustling and leg-pulling, and John McCririck, having a rant about horses not parading, both fresh from Channel 4's Morning Line. Jonathan Powell, asking this and that. It can be difficult.

When I went racing as a boy I'd see the names of journalists in the *Sporting Life* and assume that the big Bentleys and Rovers in the racecourse car park belonged to them. Later, when I got a press badge of my own, I saw my heroes in the flesh and discovered that most of them weren't the colossi I had imagined. They were more like history or geography teachers, shuffling around on feet of clay. Tony Stafford of the *Daily Telegraph* was a definite live-wire, but I hadn't been using the press room for long when he asked if he could borrow £100. And he wasn't the only one. The Bentleys didn't belong to my heroes after all.

By 11 a.m. I'm looking at the handicaps at Chester and Goodwood. Mark will be looking at spread bets at Doncaster – the indexes and the match bets – for different ways of backing my opinions. I phone him to put on some more bets, and ask David Stevens, Coral's representative, for £5,000 to £450 each-way Sierra Vista at Chester, 7-2 in my book but 11-1 in theirs. He rings the office. 'OK, mate,' he confirms.

Most of my business is done before the first race starts. It's like that on the big days, when the off-course market is very competitive. With the bets we've had in the Portland, today could be a bad day by ten past two. On average, I win on two or three days out of six. Most days are losing days, but most months are winning ones. You know you are going to have more losers than winners, but, as I said, hopefully the winners more than make up for the losers.

At a quarter to two, I go down to the parade ring. Hogmaneigh is being walked around on the grass. He looks good. Then I walk back to the grandstand and stand on the steps reserved for the press. Red, white and blue barbers' poles hold the building up, which is reassuring. There's a big, jolly crowd, women in summer dresses and lively hats. York is a lovely place to be.

I watch the race through binoculars – a rarity nowadays as most people watch the big screens. Hogmaneigh is bumped at the start of the five-and-a-half-furlong race, is immediately last of the nineteen runners, and two furlongs from home is still hopelessly off the pace. Then, as jockey Saleem Golam seeks out the gaps, weaving through, he is checked, and does well to finish third. Of course, I wish I'd backed him each-way, and I wish Fantasy Believer hadn't won. Not good. If Hogmaneigh doesn't win the Ayr Gold Cup next week, he may win the Wokingham at Royal Ascot next June. Ascot's uphill finish should suit him.

The profit and loss account makes for unappetising reading. If Wasseema wins the Park Stakes, we're in the River Ouse. We've sold her on the spreads, and laid her for a place on Betfair, at just over evens. If Somnus wins, we've won the crown jewels. As well as the £200 each-way at 25-1, we've had £333 on Betfair at 31-1. I usually bet like that: £333, £222, £111. That way you just hit the same key on the computer. It saves your fingers.

I didn't think Wasseema would be allowed a soft lead, but she is, and when she's challenged by Iffraaj, the odds-on favourite, and Somnus, she keeps on better than I expected, to finish third, which is a blow, because I've laid her for a place. It's not as big a blow as Somnus not quite getting there, after looking as if he might do half a furlong out. Iffraaj wins, Somnus second. Bollocks. Victory for him would have been worth £15,000 for us.

It could still be a ten grand day though, depending on what happens to Sixties Icon.

In the parade ring before the St Leger, I don't like the look of Jadalee, the third favourite. I don't claim to be a great paddock judge, but he looks long, lean and weak, perhaps over the top for the season, and I decide to lay him for a place.

Two furlongs out, Frankie Dettori is cruising on Sixties Icon. When I look at the others, then back to the favourite, he's a certainty to win unless he finds nothing or gets trapped in a box. Don't mess it up, Frankie. He doesn't. Thank God for that, and I played it brilliantly. I backed the winner at a good price, hedged it when it was at its shortest price, and didn't lose my bottle and lay it all off.

We've had a hell of a race here, including on our match bets. That was a £20,000 race and a £10,000 day. Actually, I think I've been quite unlucky. If Wasseema hadn't held on for third and Red Rocks ditto in the St Leger, it would have been a great day. Still, 'if' is the biggest word in gambling.

Now I'm knackered, but not too knackered to celebrate.

CHAPTER ONE

LEARNING BAD WAYS

Mark Coton, who was responsible for the launch of Pricewise in the *Racing Post* in 1987, once told me that if you are working class there are only three ways to make serious money: crime, prostitution or gambling. Since I'm clumsy and the worst liar in the world, crime is out; my arse isn't pretty, so prostitution is out too; which leaves gambling. Luckily, my mother worked in a fish and chip shop in Halifax. At lunchtimes, on the way to work, she'd drop me off at her father's. He'd sit me on his knee and tell me what he thought was going to win at Pontefract that afternoon. He was mad about racing. I was about five years old. And that was how it all started.

Evidently I could read a racecard before I could walk, and had my first bet when I was six. If my granddad had anything to do with it, the horse's form figures probably read 00000, because he was a big follower of horses with a string of ducks' eggs next to their names. He thought it meant they were due a win. I took more notice of the Lucky Jim cartoons in *The Sun*, where you had to work out what the tipster's tip was from the cartoon. If you worked it out, it made you feel as if you'd already found the winner. Unfortunately, you usually hadn't.

My granddad would spend the whole morning working out his bets. I think it was a form of occupational therapy for him. He'd start with a collection of betting slips and eventually cover them with twopenny doubles and penny trebles and accumulators. If he really fancied one, he'd have a shilling on it, but the whole lot wouldn't add up to more than 7s. 6d. – 38p nowadays. When he'd finished this work of art we'd walk down to the Ladbrokes betting shop in Nursery Lane in Ovenden, Halifax. Whether they'd let me in or not depended on which manageress was in charge. It was difficult to pretend that I was eighteen, since I was only eight.

On bank holidays, we'd pack some sandwiches and a flask and catch a Shearings coach from Halifax bus station for an outing to Wetherby or York or Ripon. At the racecourse, I'd run around the betting ring looking for the best prices for my granddad, although it didn't help much because he had his favourite bookmakers whom he'd bet with regardless of their prices. He thought they were lucky. My granddad wasn't, it must be admitted, very professional in his approach to betting.

The first horses I remember were trainer Arthur Stephenson's Celtic Gold and Supermaster, at Wetherby, and a horse called The Celestial Traveller. All three of them raced until they were thirteen years old, and I got to know them. Soon, racing was utterly engrained in me. Every week I was given a shilling's pocket money and every week I'd spend it on a shilling four-horse accumulator. It came up once, which pleased my father, because he kept most of the winnings. My father sometimes had bets with his mates, but it was my granddad who was the real racing enthusiast.

When I arrived at Highlands Grammar School I was delighted to discover that they took *The Times* and the *Daily Telegraph*. News of the latest political developments tended to pass me by, but I'd sit down and diligently study the racing pages. Then I started to buy the *Sporting Chronicle*. My local paper shop didn't stock racing papers so I used to walk two miles to one that did. During the week I got the *Sporting Chronicle*, and on Saturdays I got the *Sporting Life*, which I preferred but was more expensive. An older boy used to ask me about the day's racing, then mock me when I gave him my novice's opinion. Someone close to him worked at Timeform, whose offices were in Halifax, and he was armed with a lot of knowledge. In the end, I asked him to teach me about racing. He'd give me tests during break times. He'd ask me how good a particular horse was and, because I didn't know any better, my answer would be based on the horse's form figures. I'd no idea what handicap ratings were. I just assumed that if a horse's form read 121, it was better than one whose form read 030. Of course, that was bollocks.

The older boy's name was Paul Stansfield. He ended up working for a racecourse bookmaker, Colin Webster. Paul's knowledge of the form was fantastic, but he could still turn £1,000 into a fiver quicker than anything. After spending hours studying the form, he'd get to the races, ask someone what they fancied, and back that. For a lot of people, there's something terribly seductive about a tip, or 'information', even if it's from a down-at-the-heel trainer who can't afford to mend the hole in his jacket. The system I used had about the same chance of success. It was based on allotting ten points for each win and five for a second, and then backing the horse that had accumulated the most points. Stupid.

A bit later, my dad became friendly with someone who worked at Timeform, and the friend gave us week-old copies of the Black Book. I looked forward to getting the Black Book more than anything else in life. When it arrived, I'd open it, smell it, then pore over it. It changed me from being a granddad-type punter into a proper student of form. My interest quickly became an obsession. I used to think about the next day's racing so much that I couldn't sleep the night before.

Then my English teacher, later my form teacher, Mike Brewer, spotted my interest in racing. He was a Cambridge graduate who had somehow ended up in teaching, resented it, wasn't happy at home, and used racing as his escape. He'd catch me studying the racing pages, pretend to be taking me to task for it, but actually be asking what I fancied. Before long he was taking my bets down to the betting shop for me at lunchtimes. I suppose he was my first 'putter-on'. By the time I was in the sixth form, they were pretty hefty bets. I once asked Mike to put on a £50 win four-horse accumulator for me. In 1978, £50 was a great deal of money, especially for a working-class schoolboy. Three of the horses won and the other finished second – the traditional fate of accumulators.

My pocket money wasn't enough to pay for bets like that, so I did a milk round before school and a newspaper round after school. During the summer holidays I worked at my uncle's small machine tool factory, cleaning the machinery. I earned £7 or £8 a day, plus £2 for overtime in the evenings. It came to about £50 a week, which made me one of the richest boys at the school.

In those days, televisions weren't allowed in betting shops, which made me even keener to go racing. During term-time, every Saturday morning Mike would pick me up and drive us to a race meeting. He loved it. He was living his dream. With him, there was an enormous sense of a man who felt he had missed out in life, and this was his way of making up for it. We became real mates. I saw him recently at Carlisle, still racing, and betting.

Before we set off each Saturday, we'd call in at Ladbrokes to put our multiple bets on, then put our singles on at the racecourse. By then I was sixteen and could just about get away with putting my own bets on. There was an element of rivalry in our betting. I remember at Doncaster one Saturday in October 1978 when one of us had backed Chokwaro and the other Grand Niece, and they were fighting out the finish with both of us screaming their names. Chokwaro won by a short-head, but I can't remember which one of us backed it.

These Saturday outings weren't enough to satisfy my growing appetite for racing. During the week I had some terrible illnesses when racing was on television. Sometimes I was in such a bad way that I had to be sent home. I was a very sickly child, but somehow I managed to force myself to sit up in front of the television set. Seeing John Rickman raise his hat on ITV was the most miraculous cure. Before long I was bunking off school regularly. My parents had split up and my mum didn't have any control over me. Sometimes, when I went back to school without a note from her to explain my absence, Mike would ask, 'Did you back any winners?'

Mum used to set off for work before I left for school, which was helpful. One day, a Monday at the end of that same October, I took my duffel bag, with a change of clothes, and caught a train from Halifax to Thornaby, to go racing at Teesside Park. I won about £25, which was a lot of money for me then, so I thought I'd stay the night and go again the next day, although I knew I'd be in serious trouble when I got home. I found a seedy café in Thornaby where you could stay for £1.50. A man showed me to a tiny room with four camp beds in it. I had something to eat, then went to bed. Later on, lorry drivers started to arrive, great big blokes, pissed out of their heads. I stuffed my money down my underpants, clung on to my prize possession – my binoculars – and tried to go to sleep. But with them talking, farting and snoring, it was impossible.

The £1.50 included breakfast, but I gave that a miss. As soon as it was light, I walked to the racecourse. A few horses were being exercised and when I asked one rider the name of his horse, he said, 'Viking Spirit. He'll definitely win today.' You can imagine, that was it for me. I had £30 at 100-30. It was a hurdle race with Tommy Carmody riding and there was never a moment when Viking Spirit wasn't going to win. He won on the bridle, hard held, by five lengths. For me, the race was a dream come true, one I'll never forget. As Viking Spirit passed the post, my legs started to shake. I could hardly get down the steps to the betting ring to collect my winnings. When I did, the bookmaker was horrible to me. I could tell that he knew I was underage when I put my bet on, but he'd wanted my £30. Now he absolutely hated paying me. Every single note he handed over, he resented – a bit like Barry Dennis, who'll be cropping up later.

I didn't stop there. Silver Buck was making his chasing

debut, also ridden by Carmody, and I had £100 at 9-4 on. In those days, it seemed as if novice chasers never fell. By the time I left Teesside Park, I'd won over £200.

When I got back to Halifax I bumped into my sister and some friends of hers on the bus home. They'd been swimming. They rushed up to me, and my sister said, 'You're in real trouble now. You've done it this time. Mum's going to go mad.' 'I don't think so,' I said, pulling a wad of banknotes out of my pocket and spreading them on the seat. I was sixteen years old, they were about thirteen, and they thought it was fantastic.

When you are taller than your mother, and you've come home with what seems like a fortune, what can she say? She knew I hadn't nicked the money, and I gave her most of it. She probably didn't like what I was doing, she still worries about me betting now, but at least I wasn't robbing a bank. And, after all, it was her dad who had first got me interested. His gambling had helped keep them potless over the years, and he could see the way I was heading, but he just wanted me to get on with it. And I did.

My younger brother had a girlfriend whose father worked at Timeform and I got her to ask her dad if there were any Saturday jobs. There were, selling Timeform racecards at northern racecourses. As far as I was concerned, it was the best job imaginable. I'd have done it for nothing. You turned up at Timeform's offices at eight a.m. on Saturday morning, loaded the racecards into a van, then set off for the racecourse. I was a hopeless salesman, though. People would come up and ask if they could see what the card said about a particular horse in a race, and I'd let them. When I was on the stall, it was like a library.

We were supposed to pack up after the second race, and some of the people I was working with always wanted to get back home promptly, which I couldn't understand, because I always wanted to stay until the end. I usually managed to spin it out until after the fourth race, and sometimes I'd stay on by myself and make my own way home. I loved the atmosphere at racecourses, but it was the gambling, not the horses, that appealed to me. There were certain horses I had a soft spot for, and followed, but they meant a lot to me mainly because they'd won when I'd backed them.

When I was twelve, Tingle Creek was one of my favourites, and Pendil, who was a year older, was another. When they met at Sandown in November 1974 I was adamant that over two miles Tingle Creek would murder Pendil. Pendil won. I couldn't believe it. Two years later, on a May bank holiday Monday at Wetherby, we went to see Tingle Creek. I couldn't sleep the night before, I was so excited. I tried to sing myself to sleep: 'Super Tingle, super Tingle, super Tingle Creek'. We stood next to a fence early in the race to watch him jump. Tingle Creek was a spectacular jumper. It was an amazing sight, but he was beaten again. It was a handicap, and Tingle Creek was carrying 12st 7lb. The winner, Golden Fort, had 10st.

Tingle Creek was 9-4 on that day, but I probably had everything I'd got on him, which wasn't a very sensible approach. Two years later, I tried a different one. Every Thursday I used to get the Sporting Chronicle Handicap

Book, and on the inside cover there was always an advertisement for the Dawson System, with claims of lots of good-priced winners and enormous profits. The system cost £20. Eventually, some schoolfriends and I clubbed together and sent off for it.

When the Dawson System arrived, it turned out to be a four-page pamphlet. You had to back Split Second's selections from the *Sporting Chronicle*, putting enough on the first one to win £1. If it lost, you put enough on the second selection to win what you had lost, plus £1. When one won, you'd won £1, and you started again. It's the oldest system in the book, and to begin with it went well. That summer I saved £100 and told my uncle at the machine tool factory that I wanted to do the Dawson System professionally. He had no interest in racing or gambling at all, but, after my father left, I think he thought he was my moral guardian. He wanted me to discover the folly of my ways, so he told me to go ahead, and said he'd match my stakes. He gave me £100. A few days later, I was able to give him £65 of it back, which I think worried him a bit.

I applied the system to my own selections. The trouble was, I was still at school, so I had to back the first horse at lunchtime, guessing what price it was going to be, then dash back to the betting shop after school for the last race. Eventually the inevitable happened, and I had a string of losers.

For some reason, I decided that Hand Over Fist, the 7-2 favourite in the Kindersley Amateur Riders' Maiden Stakes at Doncaster in October 1978, ridden by Mr H. Orde-

Powlett, was the horse that was going to win me the £280 I had to win in order to get back the £279 I'd lost on the run of losers, plus £1. One of the lads from school had a car, so we all bundled in and drove to the betting shop. I put on £80, which must have equalled the rest of the shop's takings for the day. I should have known what would happen because Hand Over Fist had already finished second four times that season. He just didn't want to win, and he didn't. He was beaten three quarters of a length by a horse ridden by Tim Easterby.

That, as far as I was concerned, was the end of the Dawson System. It was a lucky escape, really. Although the system isn't sold any more, it is still alive and well, constantly reappearing in different guises, forever being discovered by some new unfortunate. People sometimes come up to me and tell me about the system and how good it is, and in a way they are right. If you have an infinite amount of money and a bookmaker who is prepared to keep taking your bets for ever then, eventually, when you have a winner, you will win back all your losses, and £1. I just say to them, 'It's an interesting system. I think it may not be new. I'd be a bit careful.' And hope they are, otherwise they'll find that their bank has disappeared before the system finally comes good.

Systems don't suit me, because you have to obey the system's rules religiously, and I'm not good at that. Anyway, the law of sod ruins most systems. That's the law that states that when the system identifies a 33-1 winner, you are in hospital visiting a bookmaker who has just broken his leg.

If anyone asked me what I wanted to be when I left

school, I told them I wanted to be a professional gambler. I wanted to be one, but I hadn't got a clue how to be one, and was nowhere near being one. I was going to be a geologist. I'd got A levels in geology and geography. But I'd also discovered drinking and girls, as well as gambling. All three had a devastating effect on my academic standards, although they did wonders for my levels of enjoyment.

Taking girlfriends racing is usually a mistake, and it certainly didn't do me much good in 1980, when I took Julie Kirkbride to the Grand National. Julie, who was quite a girl and very good looking, went to the same grammar school in Halifax as me but by this time was at Cambridge University. While she eventually went on to become a Conservative MP and Shadow Secretary of State for Culture, Media and Sport, I went on to the all-weather at Wolverhampton and Southwell.

The Grand National later became a very good race for me, particularly in 1994 when I had £3,000 on Miinnehoma at 20-1, but my early experiences weren't so enjoyable. The year before I went to Aintree with Julie I had £25 on Zongalero, some of it at 40-1. My mother thought I'd had £2. We sat in the living room and watched the race on television. I screamed my head off, but that didn't stop Rubstic outstaying Zongalero to ruin my day.

I was convinced that Zongalero would win the next year and accumulated a collection of ante-post bets, which I kept under the bunk above me in the bedroom I shared with my two brothers. I'd regularly take the betting slips out and admire them, confident that they were money in the bank. I'd backed Zongalero at about 8-1, but if I'd waited until the day of the race I could have had 11-1, because it poured with rain, the going was heavy, and Zongalero's chance disappeared in the mud. Julie and I stood in the stands, peering through the miserable gloom, and I was just able to see Zongalero, exhausted, refuse at the twentieth. There were only four finishers, led by Ben Nevis, and I don't think Julie was very impressed.

Years after our trip to Aintree, I bumped into Julie at Royal Ascot, where she was being entertained in Coral's box. I was able to remind her of her days in the backstreets of Halifax. I'm not sure if she was grateful.

Sports spread betting didn't exist in 1980, but in 2001, when it did, and conditions were even worse, I had the safest bet I've ever had on the Grand National. The rain was torrential, the track was arguably unraceable, and it was obvious that there would be very few finishers, yet Sporting Index were still quoting 12-13 as the number of finishers, from 40 starters. I sold at twelve for as much as they would accept, which was £500, and there were four finishers, two of which had been remounted. That really was easy money, although it wasn't a pleasant sight.

In 1980, my mother was working at the Halifax General Hospital, and so was a nurse called Carol. I fell in love with her, and when she said she was moving to Eastbourne, I decided to go with her. I wanted to get away from home, and away from Halifax. When my dad legged it, relatives told me that I was the head of the family, but the thought of that responsibility weighed on me. Later, I felt guilty about having left my family.

In Eastbourne, I got a job as an auxiliary nurse at Chaseley Home, a home for disabled ex-servicemen. The wage was about £32 a week – less than I'd been earning while I was still at school. We worked shifts, 7 a.m. to 2.30 p.m. or 2.30 p.m. until 10 a.m. If I was on an early shift I'd go straight from work to a betting shop and spend the rest of the afternoon there. I like to think I won; I certainly took it pretty seriously.

I liked summer jumps meetings best, backing horses like Mighty Marine, a prolific winner of chases for Milton Bradley. I used to love putting £7 on to win £2 in a novice chase, and paying tax on it. When I think about it now, it was stupid, and there were days when I was totally skint, but I was a sucker for backing odds-on shots in four-runner chases. That was what the game was all about for me. Oh dear. I had a lot to learn.

In September 1980, when that episode in my life ended, I went to Chelsea College, to study geology. My first address was on the King's Road, which pleased me, although I paid a lot more attention to what was going on in the King's Road than to what was being taught at the college. I've always been keen to make sure there was some money coming in, so on my first day I asked if there was a job going in the student union bar. After that, I think I attended only one lecture. If I was working in the bar at lunchtime, that was more or less when I got up. If I was doing an evening shift, I'd spend the afternoon in the Playboy betting shop on the King's Road.

Apart from supporting the bar, my main contribution to

the life of the college was to represent the students when the Queen Mother came to open a new hall of residence. I congratulated her on a recent winner at Sandown. Luckily she didn't ask me about my studies. At the end of my first term, my tutor informed me that there was no longer a place for me. He could find no evidence of my having done any work whatsoever – presumably because I hadn't.

I do have a social conscience, though, and every now and again think I should be a social worker. So I got a job at another home for disabled ex-servicemen and women, the Royal Star & Garter Home in Richmond. It sounds like a pub, though barmen aren't usually required to excavate their customers' rectums. Believe me, you don't want to know the details. Neither did I: I'd actually applied for a job as a kitchen porter. They weren't prepared to let me clean plates, but they didn't mind me sticking my fingers up old men's arses.

Soon after that I joined a three-year social science administration degree course at Goldsmiths College in New Cross, and managed the bar there. The most significant term was the first, when I found myself in a room full of very serious people wearing long jumpers. I quickly realised that, although to this day there is a bit of me that would like to be a social worker, my future was not working alongside them. If I was a social worker, I'd want to be paid £250,000 a year and have a lot more than four weeks' annual holiday, and that isn't going to happen. I did at least manage to stay the course. Five days before the final exams I bought one of the previous year's graduate's entire notes for a tenner and pored over them. The result was a third-class degree in sociology from

London University. It wasn't a bad result given that in my final year I gave up any pretence of studying and spent most of my time in central London, breaking off from whatever job the Manpower Agency had found for me to attend a fortnightly tutorial.

I worked for an American bank, Wells Fargo, in the West End. The people in the trading room there were racing nuts; every lunchtime it was into the pub and the betting shop. One day I told my boss, Tim Smith, that I had an important lecture I mustn't miss. Later that day, I bumped into him in the toilets at Cheltenham racecourse. Luckily he was all right about it, and we became good friends.

I also worked at a youth centre in Deptford Green for three nights a week – the result of my social conscience. A lot of the time it meant teaching West Indian kids how to fill in application forms for unemployment benefit. The centre was run by two tiny social workers in charge of huge sixteen-year-olds who were often in fights with other gangs. The centre had a panic button linked to the local police station. It had been used so many times that we were warned that if it was used again, the centre would be closed. One night I watched from the door as gangs gathered outside. There was clearly going to be Deptford's version of Armageddon, so when the youths in the centre streamed out, I screamed to one of the social workers to press the panic button. Mercifully, the police arrived quickly, and youths scattered in all directions.

That was it for me. If I'd stayed on as a full-time worker, my starting salary would have been £8,500 a year, which wasn't a lot for risking your life and however many limbs you'd still got left. With my student grant and my work in the West End, I was already making more than that.

When the course ended, three of my mates announced that they were going to Australia for a year. I decided to go with them. We lived at Randwick, near Sydney, and I used to watch the horses exercising on the racetrack there early in the morning. It didn't do me any good because I didn't know which horses were which.

I went racing every time I had a day off work, if you can call it work. I got a job on a building site, which meant joining the Builders Labourers Federation. The BLF was led by Norm Gallagher, who was a notorious character. He was one of the founders of the Maoist Communist Party of Australia, and when I arrived at the site the first thing the foreman said was that I wasn't to do any work. That suited me. They seemed to have engineered a situation where work couldn't start until at least six people were sitting around having a drink and a smoke.

We'd start work with an hour's breakfast break, then work for two hours, then have an hour's 'smoko'. If the union wasn't happy with the conditions, they'd resort to 'concretus interruptus'. We'd pour half of the required concrete into a hole, then stop. If the site manager didn't give the workers what they wanted within 30 minutes, the damage would have been done, because the concrete would have set and for some technical reason the rest of it couldn't simply be poured on top. They'd have to break up the concrete that had already set, and start again. It was a great job, sitting around in the sun, pushing a broom for a bit, and drinking tea.

The only serious exercise I did was away from the building site, preparing for the Sydney marathon. I managed that more easily than the half-marathon at Brands Hatch in 2007 – the result of too much to drink over the New Year, a big ego and a relatively small brain. I was told that I wasn't up to marathon running any more, or even half-marathon running, but I think I proved my critics wrong, although admittedly I did finish 487th and was passed by a 90-year-old lady who was sweating a lot less than me.

A few days before I was due to finish work in Australia and return to England, my union membership ran out. Unfortunately, shortly afterwards, two men-mountains turned up at the building site, came up to me and asked, 'Treating you all right in the job, mate?'

'Yes, great, thank you.'

Then they asked to see my membership card. I said I'd forgotten it.

'That's all right. Just tell us what colour it is.'

I knew it wasn't white. I guessed blue.

'Good guess, mate, but it's red. I think you'd better get off home, quickly. I'm about to shut this job down for employing non-union labour.'

A few years later, Norm Gallagher was convicted of accepting bribes from construction companies, and the union was deregistered.

By then, I was back in Britain. My first job was on another building site, at Tower Bridge. I was tired at the end of every day, which I'd never been in Australia. Then I went to a reunion for people who had worked at the Wells Fargo Bank, and ended up talking to someone who was looking for a graduate trainee dealer for a Chicago-based bank called Continental Illinois. It was the seventh biggest bank in the US, with offices all around the world, and I was to be a foreign exchange trader in London.

My five years with Continental Illinois were the best five years I ever had in a normal job. Well, fairly normal. We were supposed to be trading currencies in order to balance the bank's books, but much of the work was pure speculation, and there wasn't any proper training. Although it is never admitted, if things go wrong when trading currencies, it is the customers who lose, not the trader or the bank.

I was given a couple of minor currencies to look after. I pretended to read the *Financial Times*, just like the man who was supposed to be my mentor. He had plenty of experience, but no knowledge whatsoever. You could imagine him working at Stratford vegetable market, but not in the City. All he wanted to do was go to the pub. Our system was a bit like the Dawson System: if we got it wrong, we just doubled up and hoped it would go our way. For a while we were known as the Dangerous Brothers, and we led an amazingly charmed life. We got to the stage where we believed we knew what we were doing, but we didn't. At the end of it, I still had no knowledge of economics or currency movements.

There are two types of trader. Most are the barrow boy type, who have a feel for the way the market is moving, and move in and out to make a profit. Then there are the academic, Oxbridge graduate types who study and analyse the markets and develop a proper knowledge of them, though it doesn't always help. There was one young trader in particular, Neil, who ate the *Financial Times* for breakfast every day and knew everything. He had a brain the size of a planet, but if you asked him to trade – actually to pick up the phone and say 'yours' or 'mine' (indicating a wish to sell or buy something) – he just could not do it.

One day the chief trader from America arrived. In the States, he was in charge of 150 traders, and every year the four who performed worst were sacked. He marched around our trading room asking everyone what his trading position was, until he arrived at Neil's desk. Neil looked like a cowering schoolboy.

'What's your view, Neil? What's your position at the moment?'

Neil didn't have a position. 'I thought the markets were a bit tricky today, sir,' he said, 'so I haven't taken a position.' Neil found the markets tricky every day.

'So we're paying you, and you haven't got a fucking position?' the chief trader shouted.

Neil cowered a bit more.

'There are markets all around the world, and there's not one of them you think we should play – is that right?'

While Neil tried to become invisible, the chief trader picked up the phone, asked a broker for a price for US dollars, in German marks, and said, 'Five yours.' He'd just sold five million dollars' worth of marks. Then he turned to

Neil and said, 'You've got a fucking position now.'

Neil couldn't stand the pressure, but it never bothered me in the slightest. My mainstay was the Japanese yen. Our Tokyo office managed our yen positions until about eight a.m. our time, then we took over. There'd be a flurry of activity to start with, but if I hadn't finished work by about 9.30, which is when I started reading the *Sporting Life*, it was a seriously bad day. After that I played brokers off against one another for the privilege of paying for my lunch. The brokers were competing for our business, they had big expense accounts, and I went to a different restaurant every day for lunch, and then to a proper place for dinner in the evening. I was certainly better known for my eating, drinking and racing tips than for my trading prowess.

About three times a week the US government would release trade, employment or financial figures, and when they did it was at about 1.30 p.m. London time, which was a nuisance because we'd usually only just finished our first course. It upset me enormously, and it upset my mentor even more. His only reason for existing was to eat, drink and enjoy the pleasures of girls with big tits. It was the late 1980s, and there were plenty of people in the City like that. After six months, he was supposed to carry out an appraisal of my work. This consisted of taking me to the Cockpit in Fleet Street, getting the drinks in, then asking me what my ambitions were. I gave him the usual spiel about wanting to become a senior trader, then chief trader. He said, 'Well, you'll have to do it somewhere else, because you're not getting past me, and I'm going to sit and vegetate here for the rest of my life.'

That didn't bother me. I was enjoying the after-work programme, all paid for by the brokers. One of my favourite evening haunts was Rumours cocktail bar in Covent Garden, a natural draw for female office workers, with as much fizz as I could drink. As long as you could get up the next day and do it again, it was a terrific job and a fantastic life. I'd get back to the flat I was sharing with three friends who had all gone into accountancy and were still on about £8,000 a year, and I'd be barely able to speak because of all the champagne I'd been drinking. By then I was earning about £25,000, plus a bonus and a car, and they were seriously pissed off with me. When people say that you can't work as a trader for more than five years because of the pressure and burnout, that may be true, but in my experience the pressure and burn-out certainly weren't caused by trading currencies. What eventually made you jaded was the endless booze, birds and, in the case of some people, drugs.

I hadn't abandoned horseracing. I was still backing horses most days and going racing every Saturday. In the City, Terry Ramsden, a massive punter, was a regular in the local Mecca and William Hill shops. He was incredible to watch. It became something of a spectator sport at lunchtimes. I think he liked that. He'd write out a bet for a £5 forecast, which meant it was a £5,000 forecast, and when one went in he'd let you know; but it was also sad to watch because you knew he couldn't possibly win betting like that. There were lunchtimes when he must have lost £50,000.

Ramsden made his money on the Japanese warrants market. He'd hit on a terrific vehicle and got in at the bottom, when the market was rising vertically; but all markets eventually stop rising, and start falling. According to the City of London Police, in 1985-6 Ramsden lost £26 million gambling, another £23 million the year after, and £9 million the year after that, by which time his company, Glen International, had gone bust. At his peak, in the mid-1980s, Ramsden had over 70 horses in training, and many of his bets were based on his trainers' advice, which was ruinous.

I like to think that I was making a profit on my betting. It certainly wasn't hurting me. At that time I was very much a Timeform bettor. I'd turn up in the office with the Timeform Perspective. I wasn't really forming my own opinions, I was paying for guidance, and betting in singles and each-way doubles. Occasionally, too, a night in the City would end up at a casino, but I hate casinos. They cultivate a glamorous image, but I can't see anything glamorous about them at all. You hardly ever see a smiling face in a casino, and playing in one isn't really a social activity. I like to talk to people, and that doesn't happen much in a casino. Everyone is doing things on their own. I don't enjoy playing cards, either. I'd much rather have a drink and talk horses with someone, although I've occasionally been rounded up for a game at Cheltenham. My £50 will be the quickest to go because I haven't got a card player's face. If I've got a good hand my eyes light up with pound signs. I can't stop smiling, everyone folds, and I get my money back. It's hopeless.

I may not be able to play cards, but I did get a reputation for knowing about horses. During the afternoons, if no one was sponsoring a bar and it was deadly quiet, we'd sit in the office and study City Index's sports spread-betting screens. Brokers were always wanting tips, and it was with a mixture of brokers and old college friends that I bought my first racehorse, or a share in one. The criteria for buying a horse were that it had to be cheap and trained on the Kent side of London, so we asked a trainer called Tom Kemp, a bit of a rogue who trained at Ashford, to buy one for us. She was called Dame Flora. In September 1987 Dame Flora won an amateur riders' hurdle at Newton Abbot, ridden by Mr S. McKeever. It was my first winner as an owner, and the following August she won the three-runner Hennessy Cognac Handicap Hurdle at Southwell. God knows how they got Hennessy to sponsor the race, but we were there, like the Bash Street Kids. Dame Flora was the outsider, but Northern Ruler went lame and she just beat the favourite, Holly Buoy.

It was another horse, and a coup, that finally pushed me over the edge, hardly kicking and screaming, into being a professional punter. I had been involved with Teenage Scribbler when he was trained by Kemp. Teenage Scribbler had ability. He won a novices' hurdle at Folkestone in 1990, but he was fragile, and missed the whole of the 1991-2 season. After being pulled up at Carlisle in October 1992 he was sent to the sales. I bought him for 1,250 guineas and sent him to Karl Burke, believing that he could win a small race for us, and hopefully land a touch and win a few quid.

The race had to be a weak one, and it was: the Bridge Selling Hurdle at Catterick on Saturday, 13 February 1993, an afternoon when attention was focused on the Tote Gold

Trophy at Newbury. It must have been the worst race of the
year. There were eighteen runners and between them they
had run 53 times that season without winning a single race.
Something had to win, though, and we thought Teenage
Scribbler was good enough, and fit enough, to be the one.
Not an obvious winner in the form book, he opened at 8-1
and drifted to 12-1, possibly because my girlfriend at the
time, Lotte, hit a man with her umbrella when he approached
a bookmaker and showed signs of wanting to back our horse.
Guy Upton, not a fashionable jockey, was on board. He was
told to make all, and he did. They never got near him but it
was still a close thing, because Teenage Scribbler finished
lame. Unsurprisingly, there was no bid for him at the auction
afterwards, and he never ran again.

King Credo won the big race at Newbury, but we had
won a bigger one at Catterick: our team had been spreading
£20 bets around independent betting shops in London, and
it was worth about £100,000 to us. I was shaking with
excitement. When I rang my friend Ray, who had been
collecting his winnings, and asked him what he was going
to do with it all, he said he'd emptied a bag full of banknotes
on to the living-room floor and was rolling around in them.
It was a fantastic feeling.

That was it for me. It made me feel that I could do it. I'd
always wanted to be a professional punter, and that
November I left the City. By then I'd moved banks to Crédit
Lyonnais, with a title that suggested I was in charge of foreign
currency trading. It meant that I had people working under
me, which was a complete disaster. I was useless at man-

management, and I hated that part of the job. Whereas Continental Illinois was very active and aggressive, Crédit Lyonnais felt like working in a government post office. I'd never overworked myself, but there were people there who strolled in, picked up a piece of paper, spent the day wandering round touching each wall with it, then went home again. As for actually doing something – no. For some, it was a lifetime's retirement, before retirement.

Eventually, Crédit Lyonnais closed its City operation and I was offered a lot of redundancy money. It was perfect timing. Teenage Scribbler had paid for my and Lotte's wedding, and Lotte, who also worked at Credit Lyonnais, was terrific when I told her what I was planning to do. She had absolutely no confidence in my ability to succeed as a gambler, in fact she was convinced that I'd fail, but she took the view that there was no point me getting another job in the City and coming home every evening dissatisfied. She thought I had to get it out of my system and then return to the real world. 'When the money's gone, get yourself a job,' she told me. I don't think I was working in the real world before, and I don't think I've worked in it since.

I had £50,000 to start off with, which was almost certainly a lot more than most professional punters on the racecourse start with, but it still wasn't enough. Luckily, Lotte got another highly paid job and carried on working full time until our second child was born, when she worked part-time. I didn't really know what I was letting myself in for.

CHAPTER TWO

STEPPING INTO THE RING

To be a professional punter, you have to pay the admission fees. You make mistakes, sometimes expensive ones, and have to learn from them. You have to establish a new lifestyle, in my case very different from the old one. I was stepping on to the racecourse with huge determination, but I didn't know what I was doing.

When I left the City, I knew Timeform Perspective off by heart, and I knew Raceform, but although you may be able to make a profit by relying on them, and can certainly stop losing, I don't think it's the way to make proper money, and it was proper money I was determined to make. I hadn't left the City in order to drink tap water instead of champagne, or to live off a toilet cleaner's wage.

One of the first things I discovered was that the people who made their living on the racecourse, bookmakers and professional punters, weren't as I had imagined them to be. I had come from an industry which dealt in millions of pounds every day, and I thought the racecourse market was the same. I thought bookmakers were rich and were used to dealing in big sums, and that professional punters were betting on a huge scale, and making fortunes. I was mistaken. Despite the fact that I'd been going racing on Saturdays all my life, and on other days when I could, and was totally wrapped up in it, I was hopelessly wrong about the reality of the racecourse market.

It came as a complete surprise to me that when I went to put on £400 I could only get on £200, and that there were a lot of professional punters who would never have a bet as big as £400. For many of them, the ceiling of their ambition was to stay in the game. They set out for the racecourse hoping to win the sort of sums in a week that I'd been used to spending on one good lunch in the City, or someone spending on my behalf. Those professional punters got a buzz from the feeling that, in some way, they were putting two fingers up at society and getting away with it, even if they would have made more money stacking shelves at Tesco.

Even a successful, respected professional punter like Alan Potts was operating on a scale well below what I had in mind. In his book *Against the Crowd*, published in 1995, Potts related that his normal maximum stake was £400 and that he was not comfortable with a bet of over £500. 'My aspiration is to make an annual profit of at least £10,000,' he wrote. 'There are no fortunes to be made from full-time punting, but there is a steady income for the hard working and the competent.' To me, that sounds depressing, a vision of hard labour rewarded by baked beans on toast. Although we are chalk and cheese in terms of our personalities – Potts actually calls his racehorse ownership venture The Golden Anorak Partnership – I am not criticising his knowledge or approach. We all have to bet in the way that suits us best, but in my view, if you make only £10,000 a year from betting then you are not really a professional punter because you would be considerably better off doing almost anything else for a living. You have not beaten the system and must be living a pretty quiet life, probably in a bus shelter.

Three years earlier, in 1992, Nick Mordin published *Betting for a Living*. Mordin was forever developing and testing different betting systems and I loved his book, but his ambition was as limited as Potts. Mordin admitted, 'My emotional threshold for betting is about £100. When I bet beyond that amount I start to get jittery and my judgement goes.' At a time when he had plenty of money in the bank, Mordin once had a bet of £200. 'I was having kittens as the dead cert skipped home,' he recalled. Mordin set out to prove, as the title of his book suggested, that you can bet for a living, but during the six months of his experiment he made an average of only £1,100 a month, which he estimated worked out at £8 per hour of work. That wasn't the kind of living I had in mind.

Mordin and Potts may well be making a lot more nowadays but I still see people eking out a living at the racecourse. I think a lot of them are loners and misfits, and women don't figure in their lives at all. Apart from Eddie Fremantle and me, I can't think of any professional punters on the racecourse who are married, with children.

I was attracted to the racecourse by the colour and buzz and excitement, but soon realised that other professional punters, although we shared a common interest, were very different. I thought of the racecourse as a place for having a good time – a bit of betting, a bit of drinking, a bit of fun. Yet the professional punters I met seemed to be very serious and insular. They included people I still talk to and respect, but, while they don't look unhappy, I wonder what makes them content. The City's trading rooms had been very different, full of noisy people with big egos, where it was a lot of fun and everyone took the piss out of one another.

Maybe racecourse traders were more cerebral than me. They certainly went home straight after racing and started studying the next day's card. That's not an image I'd like to have of myself. I like the image of being happy and successful in my work. If I've got sunken eyes, it's more likely to be because I've been out until four a.m. celebrating a win than because I've been studying the form all night. I think that irritates some people.

Having said that, the problem for me, as for them, was and is that the job is so time-consuming. The travelling means that you have to get up early every day to start studying the day's card. There is no other life.

The first day of this new life was 11 November 1993, the day I set out for the betting ring. It wasn't a great start. A skinhead spat at me on the train, we had a wrestling match on Farringdon station, and I then spent two hours in a police station. I did eventually get to Towcester, but I don't remember anything very successful happening while I was there.

Jump racing was my thing, and the Flat season had just ended. The question was, how was I going to make it pay? I thought it was simply a case of backing more winners than losers, and that the way to do that was to find one really solid bet each day, two at the most, and have a fairly big bet on it, say £500 to £2,000. The aim was to have a small number of big bets, with a high percentage of winners, most of which would be at odds of between 6-4 and 9-4. A lot of them would be favourites in novice hurdles and small-field chases.

There were two problems with this. The first was that I

hadn't realised what an action junkie I am. One or two bets a day wasn't enough to satisfy my need for action. I started out by being very methodical and mechanical. I read the *Sporting Life* from cover to cover, and Timeform Perspective, selected one or two solid horses, and drove to the racecourse to back them. At that time there were still 9 per cent deductions off-course, so you had to bet on-course. That was fine, as long as my banker of the day won. Provided it won, I was the most disciplined gambler in the world, and I believed that discipline was the key to success. The horse would win, and I'd happily stand and watch the other races without having a bet. The problem came when the horse got beaten, especially if I was a long way from home. The further from home I was, the more determined I was to win the money back, and more. It's not easy to be content with having put in a twelve-hour day, and done your bollocks, but it's worse when you start chasing your losses, lose more and start talking to yourself, gnarling, gritting your teeth and clenching your fists. Then I'd have to drive home.

It was on days like that that I most missed the City. I'd ring up some of the boys and arrange to meet up for a drink, so that I could talk to someone else who'd had a bad day. Every morning I was stepping out with determination but without huge confidence, because I didn't really know what I was doing. I was spending my redundancy money and getting seriously angry with myself because it soon became clear that I wasn't the successful professional punter I was supposed to be, and no one was to blame but me.

The second problem was that I wanted to make enough

money to enable Lotte to stop working. I'd read about professional punters making between 2 and 3 per cent profit on their turnover. If I was betting £12,000 a week, even if I made 5 per cent profit, that would bring in only £600 a week, which wasn't bad until you knocked off the expenses, which were £200 to £250 a week. The sums just didn't add up. Either I had to be much more successful than other people in terms of my percentage profit, or I had to turn over a hell of a lot more. But I didn't have the bottle to have £5,000 bets, and I didn't have enough £5,000s to do it anyway, even if I found the bottle.

Something had to change, or Lotte's prediction would soon come true: I'd be looking for a real job. I've got Eddie Fremantle to thank for managing to avoid that.

Eddie, known as 'Eddie the Shoe', was a racing journalist with the *Racing & Football Outlook* and then the *Sporting Life* who had just left the paper to become a full-time professional punter. He'd already been successful on a part-time basis and was finding that it cost him money to carry on working as a journalist. Eddie is still a successful professional punter, active at the racecourse where, like me, he's now also seen on Racing UK. We met while travelling on the same trains to the same race meetings, and discovered that we lived very near to each other, Eddie in Putney and me in Wandsworth. Eddie always wanted to go home when the racing ended, even if we were racing at Newton Abbot and it was Taunton the next day; as time went on, I liked to stay overnight, discover new people and places, and have an excuse for having a good time. Maybe that's why Eddie's still married.

Eddie was someone I thought I could learn from, and he told me how he operated. He produced a 'tissue' for each race, pricing up every horse based on his view of each horse's chance of winning. It was his own version of the forecast odds for races that newspapers produce, but without the bookmakers' profit margin built in. Eddie then compared his prices with the ones available from bookmakers in the betting ring, and backed the horses that were being offered at significantly longer prices in the ring. They were the ones Eddie believed represented that elusive concept, 'value'.

It was so obvious I couldn't believe that I'd never considered doing it myself, especially since it was a system that suited me. I like a statistical approach, and I'm very good, and quick, at mental arithmetic, at assimilating figures and working out odds and percentages. I'm good at spotting prices that are out of line.

So Eddie the Shoe got me going. Within nine months of starting at the racecourse I was using his approach. It's how I've operated ever since, and I think it's the way to do it. I've reached the conclusion that if you just try to pick winners you can't win, but if you play the percentages, you can. If you just back the horses you fancy, which is what most punters do, you will eventually go skint, because most of the time your selection's chance of winning will be pretty accurately reflected in its price, and the price includes a profit margin for the bookmaker. You can only win if you are a consistently better judge of what a horse's true chance is, and what its odds should be, than the market, and you bet accordingly. Otherwise, the margins will get you in the end.

As soon as I changed my approach, I started to go racing feeling confident that I was odds-on to win, every day. I'd pick one meeting a day — that was enough for me — and concentrate on those six or seven races. Very often I decided where to go the next day after buying the *Evening Standard* on the way home. Nowadays I like the big meetings best, but Eddie told me that the value lay at the small meetings, which may well have been the case in those days.

I wanted to go to meetings where there were handicaps for older horses rather than maiden races or novice hurdles, because I don't back horses on information and never have done. I like to study the form, and there isn't much form in races for maidens and novices.

Before I saw the light, or Eddie introduced me to it, I would look for a horse I fancied strongly, then have a big bet on it at, say, 6-4. After my conversion, I looked for horses whose odds were at least 15 per cent better than the price I thought they should be, and backed those. It didn't matter what horse I fancied in the race, or which horse I thought would win, or not win, because every horse has some sort of chance of winning, whether a very good chance or an extremely remote one, and my view of its chance was built into the price I allotted it. In my tissue, I might have one horse at 2-1 favourite and another at 10-1. If the best prices for them on the racecourse were 2-1 and 16-1, I'd back the 16-1 shot, even though I thought the 2-1 favourite was much more likely to win. It was more likely to win, but in my view it wasn't value, whereas the other horse was. If my judgements were correct, and I got the prices right, then over time I'd make money. What it amounts to, really, is a conviction that I can beat the market in assessing what the true winning chances of each horse are.

Most punters don't look at races in that way. They are always trying to pick the winner. When a punter approaches me, he always wants to know what I fancy. That's the most frequent question I am asked: 'What do you fancy?' The punter always wants me to name the horse I think will win, and if I don't tell him he feels frustrated; yet the honest answer to his question is that I don't fancy anything until I know what price it is, and how that price compares with the price in my tissue. In fact, I try not to consider what I fancy at all until I've done my tissue, because fancying something gets in the way. Making a profit on a race is very different from tipping the horse you think is likely to win, but that is a concept most punters find difficult to grasp. They either can't grasp it or don't want to, so I get slagged off for not tipping winners.

My new system, Eddie's old one, meant that I was often backing several horses in one race, which was a novel experience and quite a shock to start with, but it worked. Previously, I'd reached the stage where I was making money but only enough to cover my expenses. Now I started to make a profit after expenses – not a huge profit, but a profit – and it was no harder to get my bets on with bookmakers than it had been before, easier in some ways. That was because, instead of backing just one horse in a race, I might back three horses, with three different bookmakers. Even if one of the three horses won, two bookmakers would have won money from me. I was laying out between £3,000 and £5,000 a day, spread over six races. There were so many bets with so many bookmakers that there was less chance of being knocked back.

So the system was working fine, and I felt that I would never need financial help from anyone ever again. I wish it had been that straightforward.

Since I lived fairly near Lingfield, where they stage all-weather racing, I eventually decided to concentrate on that. At that time, other professional punters concentrated on jumps racing, which was what I'd focused on to start with, but I thought I might have an edge specialising in moderate all-weather races, as well as save myself a lot of time and money travelling.

My new system quickly produced some strange experiences, and a few disasters. In one eleven-runner sprint I'd got the 5-2 favourite in at 10-1 on my tissue, which meant that most of the others were shorter prices in my book than they were in the betting ring, so I ended up backing eight horses. Effectively, I was laying the front three in the market, pre-Betfair. I backed eight horses and didn't have a single one in the first three, which must be a record but doesn't pay very well, and makes you feel a complete chump. In those early days I was guilty of wanting to get every favourite beaten. The favourite is still the first horse I look at, and I still look at it with a view to seeing how it might be beaten, but I used to see things that weren't there, persuade myself that it was going to get beaten, for no good reason, then watch it win on the bridle.

Short-priced horses can be good value, but it doesn't suit me to have big bets on them. I've got a choking point about backing short-priced horses for big amounts, which I don't think is a bad thing. I can have £1,000 on an 8-1 shot without batting an eyelid, but I can't have £4,000 on an even-money shot without visiting the toilet. I don't like having more than a grand on a short-priced favourite, and if that's a failing, it's a better failing than that of the average betting shop punter, who will have a monkey (£500) on an even-money shot but only risk £20 on a 10-1 shot. I'd rather be the other way round.

The problem for me is a mental one. If I back a short-priced horse and it gets beaten, and I see the smile on the face of the bookmaker who has just taken my grand, I beat myself up over it. I think, how badly did you need to win £800 to be throwing £1,000 away to do it? I never think that if I've had £840 to £60, and the bet loses.

The trick is to press up on the longer-priced horses that you think represent good value. You may fancy an 8-1 shot as much as an even-money shot, but most punters will still have a bigger stake on the even-money shot. Ideally, the thing to do is not to back the even-money horse at all, just the 8-1 shot, or at least have the same stake on both.

With experience, I gained the confidence to have bigger bets on longer-priced horses, even on horses that were drifting in the market. Year after year, I found that some of my most successful bets were on horses that I'd busted a gut to take an early price on, with people running around for me to get 7-1 in the morning, only to find that the horse was

10-1 at the track in the afternoon. That sets alarm bells ringing for punters. Before betting exchanges arrived, I'd feel gutted. After exchanges arrived, I'd feel gutted and suspicious, wondering if something sinister was happening? Especially at big meetings where you can fairly safely assume that every jockey is trying to win, I decided the thing to do was to have more on. If you believe that a horse is good value at 7-1 then, logically, it must be even better value at 10-1. I have often won five-figure sums pressing on in those situations, and it doesn't scare me any more. It is very easy to be put off horses that drift in the market and very hard to stay with them, but if after having another look at the reasons you thought 7-1 was good value, you still think your reasons are valid, you have to put more on.

Whatever you do, you have got to gamble in a way that suits you, and my new system suited me. It satisfied my need for action, effectively giving me a fix every half an hour, which is what I need. I'll have more bets in a day than some professional punters will have in a season. Steve Mellish, for instance, who also writes for the *Racing & Football Outlook*, and appears regularly on Racing UK, is someone I respect enormously, but he'll have a fraction of the bets I have. I don't know how he does it. He'll watch races with tremendous enthusiasm but without backing anything. 'I'm not going to have a bet on this race,' he'll tell the viewers – nor on this one, nor on this one, nor on this one. I watch racing on television because it's helpful for my job, but unless I'm financially involved, I can't pretend that I find it interesting. Without the involvement of money it's largely just horses going round in circles. I can't get enthused about a horse who has just run a good trial for the Ebor.

I have always been much more risk-oriented and financially ambitious than most of my contemporaries, and most professional punters. Lotte and I had both been used to having high salaries. Within about four years of becoming a professional punter, I was making about £50,000 a year – a grand a week, in cash, tax free. That's good money, but it still wasn't as much as I'd been making in the City, and I kept thinking about how much more I'd be making if I'd stayed there. It was open to question, and a worry for Lotte, whether or not we and the children would be able to maintain our lifestyle. We were living a decent life, but I didn't think I'd proved myself. I was still only one or two bad months away from being skint and was so paranoid about failure – which it's easy to be when you don't have a salary cheque coming in every month – that I absolutely immersed myself in betting.

I tried my best to be a reasonably attentive father, but there wasn't a moment in the day when I wasn't thinking about betting. My old friends soon discovered a new me, one who didn't have a comment on anything and could barely recall the Prime Minister's name. There was little going on in my head outside betting. Now and again I might briefly re-establish contact with the outside world, but if you caught me on the wrong day, you could talk to me as much as you liked and get nothing back. I might be looking at you but nothing was going in, which frustrated the hell out of people close to me. At dinner parties, people who were used to me making conversation and wisecracks, and expected it, found that I was just nodding and smiling, because I was somewhere else.

I've certainly experienced the obsessive aspect of gambling, been as guilty as most in becoming wrapped up in racing and allowing it to take over my life. Yet I haven't lost friends as a result, and it's one of the things I am most pleased about. Even when I was totally absorbed in trying to make a success of gambling, I maintained my friendships. Four times a year, I'd meet up with old university friends who had no interest whatsoever in racing or betting and have a booze-up in the City, and they were occasions I'd particularly look forward to. Day by day, though, I would come home, read whatever I hadn't already read in the *Racing Post* or *Sporting Life*, which wasn't much, play with the kids for an hour, then sit down at my desk with the recordings of the racing on television, and start studying again. There wasn't anything else.

★

I think the only prisoners who haven't escaped from Ford Open Prison, near Arundel, are the ones who enjoy their trips out to Fontwell races, and would miss them. An Old Fordonian was one of the motley crew with a share in National Flag, the horse supposed to provide an encore to Teenage Scribbler's lucrative coup – the horse who had given me the kick I needed to swap the City for the racecourse.

At the end of 1993 a group of four of us bought National Flag, a once-raced three-year-old from John Oxx's yard in Ireland, and sent him to Karl Burke's yard, which was then in Wantage. In his first two hurdle races, at Plumpton and

Hereford, the latter a seller, National Flag was pulled up. It wasn't a very encouraging start. The only consolation was that he had the perfect form figures for a coup, PP.

In August 1994, National Flag's stablemate, Northern Trial, won two hurdle races and Karl reported that National Flag was working as well as Northern Trial and might be good enough to win a small race. All we had to do was find a race tiny enough for him to win. We found a very small one at Worcester, a novices' selling hurdle, and agreed that we'd have £2,000 or £3,000 on National Flag, none of it with major bookmakers, and not more than £20 per bet, spread around the country – the usual thing. I got my money on, all at SP.

I had a feeling that it would be a cock-up, and it was. The first sign of trouble came when my brother phoned to say that he'd just been into a William Hill shop and the manager had told him to fuck off. Then other people rang me to ask if I'd had any trouble getting on, because they had. Eddie Fremantle, who wasn't involved in the coup but was at Worcester that day, said that one back-row bookmaker put National Flag up at 20-1, and was immediately swamped. Every other bookmaker opened up at 3-1, which isn't the price you expect a horse with the form figures PP to be. National Flag drifted to 11-2 and was then backed in again to 3-1 favourite. It wasn't what we had in mind at all, but Ladbrokes were clearly determined that our coup horse wasn't going to start at longer odds than that.

Rodi Greene rode National Flag and, after Creagmhor fell two out, he won by three and a half lengths. At the auction afterwards, we bought the horse back for the princely sum of 2,900 guineas, which was more than he was worth. He never won again.

Meanwhile, I was left staring at a pile of £20 betting slips thinking, I've got to go to all these shops, to pick up £80 at each one. It seemed as if every time I walked into a shop, someone behind the counter would shout, 'Here he comes!' As the manager was paying me out, he'd say, 'There you are, son. They're on to you now. It works once, it doesn't work a second time. We've got your number.' I almost wished that Creagmhor hadn't fallen but had won instead.

The problem was that everyone wanted too much on and they over-egged the pudding. People lied about how much they'd put on. There were four partners in the horse, I had about ten people putting on for me, and the others probably had the same. Since then, I have never laid a horse out with a coup in mind. You may be surprised by that, because I've owned a lot of horses and parts of horses, but the experience with National Flag taught me that it isn't worth it. So many things can go wrong, and often do. Although I've had some cracking wins backing horses I've owned, I've never landed another carefully planned coup. Nowadays, my version of a coup is when you enter a horse for a race and suddenly discover that it is *the* race, because everything happens to be right for your horse: the track, the going, the distance, the opposition, the weight, the likely shape of the race. Some people seem to think that owning racehorses is like belonging to an expensive club where the members agree among themselves who is going to win, but if it ever was like that, it certainly isn't any more. Gambles go wrong all the time.

The same year that National Flag failed to make me rich, 1994, so did the first tipping service I was involved with. Racing clubs were popular at the time, I was beginning to be known, and the Prestige Racing Club asked me to provide a telephone tipping service for them. They had a moderate horse called Self Expression, trained by Lynda Ramsden, who'd won a race for them at Carlisle that June, and I seemed to spend my time telling subscribers how Self Expression was going on the gallops, and taking a long time to give tips. It wasn't an experience I am proud of, but I certainly behaved a lot better than Sonny Purcell, and cost subscribers a lot less than Purcell cost me.

At the end of 1995, in a blaze of publicity, Purcell launched SP Racing, offering low-tax betting and other special offers, including tea and toast. The last thing you'd want is tea and toast with Sonny Purcell, but I must have been greedy, because I foolishly opened an account with him. One fateful day I had a £500 each-way double with SP Racing. Betfair hadn't arrived yet so, after the first leg went in, at 7-1, I made sure of a profit by backing several horses against my selection in the second leg. My selection romped home, leaving me owing several bookmakers quite a lot, and Purcell owing me a lot more. I paid the bookmakers, but Purcell either couldn't or wouldn't pay me.

I tried to be decent about it, and for a while he kept assuring me that he was going to pay. Eventually I went to his betting shop, in Harrow. The cashier was a nice young man who obviously didn't realise what he had got himself into, and was standing behind the counter trying to dodge the bullets from disgruntled punters, including me. He told me I could have everything they'd got, which was about 57p.

When he started, Purcell had appeared on Channel 4's Morning Line with John McCririck, which was useful publicity. When McCririck discovered what had happened, to his credit he got me on the programme and we issued an open plea to Purcell to pay up. There was no response. I didn't think there would be, but at least it made people, including me, aware that they needed to be careful about who they bet with.

In the end, I took Purcell to Tattersalls Committee, which deals with betting disputes. He turned up with his children, bright as can be, shook my hand and asked how I was getting on, then said I'd been abusive in his shop, which I probably had been, although it hadn't done me any good. Nor did going to Tattersalls. I ended up paying a fee of several hundred pounds for the privilege of being informed that Purcell still owed me £13,500, which I knew already. There was no chance of getting my money. If ever there was a case for bookmakers being required to put up a bond before they are issued with a licence, Purcell was that case. As far as I could see, he didn't have any knowledge of bookmaking nor, apparently, any money. Early in 1997 he finally had his licence revoked and was warned off by Tattersalls, still owing me £13,500, customs and excise £22,000, and thousands more to other customers.

By the time I'd decided to concentrate on all-weather

racing, jump racing on all-weather tracks had been abandoned. It had started on 1 November 1989, at Southwell, two days after the first all-weather Flat meeting, at Lingfield, but a string of fatalities early in 1994 brought it to an abrupt end. Richard Muddle, Southwell's boss, didn't mince his words. 'Some of the horses are not in a sound condition to race,' he said, 'and can't jump properly, but I can't stop trainers running horses here even if I think them incompetent, cruel or dishonest.' Some trainers were certainly that. In my view, all-weather jump racing was out-and-out crooked, and I think all-weather racing generally has always had a greater degree of 'iffyness' about it than turf racing.

A few years ago, when I thought the problem had got worse and I wrote about a couple of bad examples of non-triers, I had writs for libel issued against me. There have been times when I've known that a race in which I've had a bet was hooky, and that I've been mugged. That can be a problem with my approach to betting, because I operate on the basis that races are straight. If they are not, I am sunk. A horse that's drifting in the market may represent terrific value, based on its form, but it's not going to do me any good if the jockey isn't trying to win.

Banded racing made things worse. Introduced in 2004 as part of regional racing, banded stakes races were for horses with handicap ratings of 45 or below – in other words, bad horses. It gave their connections an unfamiliar chance to win some prize money, although not much, and it gave them an obvious opportunity to make money betting, crookedly. A horse that had previously struggled to get into a race at all, let alone win one, might now be first or second favourite in a dire contest, a position in the market that dishonest connections could exploit by laying the horse on a betting exchange, then making sure that it lost.

From a public relations point of view, banded racing was the worst invention ever. It was an open invitation to skulduggery, though I find it difficult to blame anyone who accepted the invitation. Viewed from a purely financial perspective, going crooked was the sensible way to go. Attendances at regional racing meetings were tiny and the betting market was very weak, so a horse's connections couldn't have a touch by backing their horse to win, because the price would instantly collapse. It was absolutely no surprise to me that the biggest touches were landed when short-priced favourites were beaten. People might have been doing things that were morally wrong and against the rules, but if racing is a business, that was the inevitable consequence of running races at that level. What made it even more of a nuisance, from my point of view, was that horses sometimes graduated from banded racing to the dizzy heights of races for horses rated up to, say, 60, which meant that I had to pay attention to banded racing when I didn't want to.

Eventually, I did pay less and less attention to all-weather racing, but that was later. For the time being, I spread my net more widely, travelling the country in search of value.

CHAPTER THREE

FLYING INTO CHRISTMAS

It will soon be Christmas 2006, and I'm in terrific, unbelievable form. I'm flying. For the last fortnight, I've been winning an average of about £6,000 a day. When I'm in that kind of form, I think it's never going to end. I think I've cracked it. And I have, until the good run ends, as good runs always do. Pity.

Recently, I've hardly been playing on Betfair at all. I still check the prices on every race, but the odds for the horses at the front end of the market are no different from the prices in the ring, and the horses at the back end of the market just don't win. In the old days, if I'd got a horse at 20-1 on my tissue, and it was available at 60-1 on Betfair, it meant it was good value, and I'd back it. Now, horses at those prices just don't seem to win, and there's been a terrific run of winning favourites recently. It may just be one of those runs, a short-term thing, but not necessarily. The markets are now dictated by the betting exchanges, which means they are set by some of the cleverest people in the game, so they are likely to be more accurate predictors of the results than the traditional market.

I've also had a good run on match bets in jump races, with the matches often making up to the maximum of fifteen lengths. One of the things I like about match bets is that you are taking on another human being, the odds compiler at a spread betting firm, rather than the giant collective brain of Betfair's market. I think that gives me a better chance. The compiler only has to get one match wrong, and I'm in, provided I spot it, and can get on.

Today I'm going to Ascot for a prime December jumps

meeting. It's nine a.m. and I'm already in the new press office. So is the nice lady who serves coffee and biscuits. I've studied the two big, sixteen-runner-plus handicaps, the Silver Cup Chase and the Ladbroke Hurdle, and haven't unearthed any great surprises. I like Harris Bay at around 11-2 and Graphic Approach at 7-1 in the former, both progressive horses, and will definitely be against Tarlac, the 4-1 favourite, in the latter. I can't see what Tarlac's done to justify such a short price.

More study, and at 9.45 I ring Coral and have £900 each-way Harris Bay at 11-2, £400 each-way Graphic Approach at 7-1, and two in the Ladbroke: £450 each-way Kings Quay at 10-1 and £550 each-way Overstrand at 9-1. Then I round it off with four £100 each-way doubles.

My appetite for betting increases when I'm having a good run. It boosts your confidence, and your bank balance. I'm feeling hungry. I want to lay Mick Fitzgerald. He's been a brilliant jockey, but he's retiring at the end of the season, and I think he's gone on for one year too long. Once a jockey has decided to retire, he will surely be more likely to have self-preservation in mind, particularly in novice chases, and look after himself. That's my theory, anyway, and I arrange for friends to sell Mick Fitzgerald on one of the spread betting firm's jockeys' index.

In the Long Walk Hurdle, I'll be against Neptune Collonges. I think Paul Nicholls' horse wants bottomless ground to show his best, he's slow, and he's returning to hurdles from fences. Also, the yard's horses maybe aren't in quite as good form as they were a while ago. My angle on the race is that Neptune Collonges, who will be second favourite to Mighty Man, will be out of the frame. I don't want to back Mighty Man at odds-on, and I think Fire Dragon, who was only three lengths behind Mighty Man in the World Hurdle at Cheltenham in March, on the same terms, is the best value at about 12-1. Tony McCoy is on him today. He's won on four of the seven occasions he's ridden Fire Dragon, and been runner-up once, so McCoy is the right man for the horse.

10.15. I phone Neal Wilkins, Victor Chandler's representative, and ask for £5,000 to £400 each-way Fire Dragon. He asks me to ring their Gibraltar headquarters. I ring and ask for £10,000 to £800 each-way, expecting to have the bet halved. They accept the lot.

Then I'm on the phone to my betting partner Mark Smith, to 'Yarmouth Andy', and to a few others, to get some match bets going. I've taken Tamarinbleu over Crozan in the first, even though Crozan is supposed to be flying at home. He probably is, but the fact is that Crozan has pulled up in his last two races, and it's not often that a PP in a horse's form figures is followed by a 1, unless the horse is called National Flag. Tamarinbleu looks pretty solid. Crozan is 2-1. I don't think you'd make much of a profit backing horses with form figures PP, at 2-1. In the same race, I've taken It Takes Time over Briery Fox, because although It Takes Time is a Grand National horse, and this race is over a much shorter distance, about two and three quarter miles, he'll get round and I think will be good enough to beat Briery Fox, who I don't rate, and who is ridden by Mark Bradburne. I like to oppose Bradburne in match bets because I think he has a tendency to ease up on horses more than most jockeys. As well as Crozan, I've opposed another of Fitzgerald's rides, Copsale Lad, who was also pulled up last time.

More phone calls, more playing on the spreads and laying on Betfair, then I write 250 words for the World Bet Exchange's website, a job I started doing in November, five days a week. It doesn't take long when you are immersed in each day's cards.

Through my various associates, I'm trying to do match bets for £100 a length, but am often having to accept £50. My approach would seem casual to a lot of punters, because if I've found a horse I want to be against, ideally in a match with a horse I fancy, I don't care very much whether the spread is, say, 0-1.5 lengths or 2.5-4 lengths. I'll be against a horse because I think the circumstances are against it and, if I'm right, the match bet is quite likely to make up at the maximum of fifteen lengths, especially if the ground is soft.

The 2007 Cheltenham Festival is now only three months away, and I've already had my ante-post bets. I'm not generally a big ante-post bettor, because of the fear of non-runners, but if you are going to have an ante-post bet for the Festival, now is the time to have one. There's no point waiting until a horse has had its final pre-Cheltenham run, perhaps in February, because it's all over from an ante-post point of view by then. The market won't change much after that, unless a horse is injured or sick.

Although my forays into the ante-post market are limited, my biggest win on a single race, so far, was an ante-post bet at Cheltenham. After Rooster Booster won a handicap hurdle impressively at Cheltenham in November 2002, I quickly had £20,000 on him to win the Champion Hurdle, at 14-1. Later, I had another £10,000, at around 10-1, and laid the favourite, Rhinestone Cowboy. As I had also backed Best Mate for the Gold Cup at 8-1, immediately after he had won the 2002 version, 2003 was a very enjoyable Festival for me. This time I've had £10,000 on Detroit City at 5-1 for the Champion Hurdle and £10,000 on Kauto Star at the same price for the Gold Cup. I'm hoping that by the day of the race both of them will be shorter prices and I'll have the option of getting out with a profit or at least protecting part of my stake.

11.40. Another phone call. I tell my friend, 'I've just emptied your Spreadex account. Can I empty your IG account?' I've sold Tarlac on Spreadex's 50-30-20-10 index, £60 at 12, and bought Billyvoddan, an outsider in the Silver Cup Chase, for the same amount at 6. Now I'm selling amateur jockey David England on a jockeys' index. I'm trying to sell for £100 at 15, but have only got £50 so far. It's an index where the jockey scores 25 points for a winner, 10 points for a second, and 5 points for a third. England has five mounts, but I don't fancy any of them. I phone Frank, one of my putters-on, to see what he can get on. And I buy another jockey, Leighton Aspell.

12.35 p.m., the scheduled time for the first race. On Betfair, I have £777 on Tamarinbleu at 2.12 and £333 on It Takes Time at 9.6. I seriously don't want Crozan to win, and he doesn't, but it's a very nervous start. Tamarinbleu just gets back up near the line to beat Crozan by a short-head. What a relief!

I look back down the course to see what's happened to It Takes Time and Briery Fox in my match bet. Both are a long way behind the leaders. It Takes Time finishes four lengths in front of Briery Fox, but it would have been more if Mark Bradburne had eased down as much on Briery Fox as Timmy Murphy did on It Takes Time. That's one of the frustrations of match bets, although sometimes it works in your favour. It helps to get to know which jockeys tend to ease down most on beaten horses.

There isn't time for much reflection, which is probably just as well. I go down the elevator to the ground floor of the spectacular but controversial new grandstand, and walk over to the pre-parade ring. Ardaghey looks fantastic, which doesn't thrill me, because he's one of David England's mounts, and I've sold him in a jockeys' index.

I wander across to the sunken parade ring behind the stand, and then through to the betting ring at the front. All those familiar faces on the rails: George Simmons and Colin Webster, in his trilby; John Christie, son of Roy, who died recently; and Geoff Banks, the son of another well-known racecourse bookmaker, John Banks. It was John Banks who once famously described betting shops as 'a licence to print money', a description that, with the arrival of fixed odds betting terminals, could be applied again in recent years.

Billyvoddan wins the Silver Cup Chase at 25-1, which is a terrific result for me, but Tarlac finishes second in the Ladbroke, which is less disastrous than if he'd won, but isn't welcome. I feel fed up about it because when you say that one can't win, bet accordingly, and it almost does win, it's not a good feeling. Even so, I'm probably a couple of grand up overall. On a day like this, I never really know exactly how I stand at any particular time, because Mark will have been putting some bets on, I don't know how much we've managed to get on, and there have been a lot of bets.

Meanwhile, I have £1,000 each-way on Oscar Park at 4-1 in the 2.05 at Haydock, a handicap hurdle. I think it's pretty much a bet to nothing, with Oscar Park having a good chance of winning and looking rock solid for a place. He starts at 7-2, and falls at the third hurdle. I swear. What else can you say?

Fire Dragon blows out completely in the Long Walk Hurdle and is virtually pulled up, but I was right about Neptune Collonges, who finishes almost eleven lengths behind Mighty Man.

It looks as if it's going to be a nothing day, unless either Mick Fitzgerald or David England have a winner, to send my jockeys' index bets the wrong way, but they don't. After Crozan's second place in the first race, Fitzgerald just has a third place on Temoin, with his other three rides unplaced, while all five of England's mounts are out of the frame. Nothing against England, but, good.

I step into the ring for the 2.45, the novices' hurdle, and have £2,000 to £1,000 on Ringaroses with William Hill on the rails, and £1,500 to £800 with George Simmons on the same horse. When Ringaroses does the decent thing, and we tot it all up, I've won almost £3,500 on the day. Messy, frenetic, but not bad for a few hours' work.

CHAPTER FOUR

AN ALTERNATIVE BRITAIN

In the early days, when I still had my old company car, I used to drive to race meetings. Then I switched to trains. Now I've got into the habit of going racing by train, and I enjoy it. At least, I enjoy long journeys. I could happily make the trip from King's Cross to York every day, but I hate the first and last legs of the journey, between home, in Kent, and London. When I can, I stop off at Waterloo station. Sadly, the nearby pie and mash shop I used to visit is now a Thai restaurant, but at least the Hole in the Wall is still there – one of London's last remaining proper pubs. Lovely.

When I was concentrating on all-weather racing, a lot of my journeys were to Southwell and Wolverhampton. If I'm going to Southwell, I'll get a train from King's Cross to Newark, then a taxi to the racecourse. If there's time, I like to stay for a while in Newark. I'll walk around the market, buy a couple of pork pies and a piece of Stilton, then go to a fantastic little café I discovered. It is like Aladdin's Cave. I make my way up its narrow stairs, taking care not to knock over the ornaments that line the stairway, into a small room where you can have a terrific breakfast, with as much tea as you can drink, for £2.95.

The obvious hotel to stay in at Southwell is the Saracen's Head, but I think it's awful, and the pubs I've stayed in as an alternative have been run by alcoholic landlords who want to stay up drinking until four in the morning. Even I baulk at that on a Monday night. Instead, I stay at a bed and breakfast place called the Old Forge, in Burgage Lane, which is much better. The first time I knocked on the door, it turned out that the lady's husband had dropped dead a few hours earlier, but she still welcomed me in, which must have taken some doing. It's a lovely place, with comfortable beds and great breakfasts.

Unfortunately, the same delights aren't on offer at Wolverhampton. In my experience, the trains from Euston to Wolverhampton are prone to delays and cancellations, possibly because even they can't face the prospect of finding themselves in Wolverhampton, which is unremittingly grim. I've stayed in some absolute khazis there. For seriously awful accommodation, Wolverhampton is hard to beat.

The Quality Hotel is horribly misnamed. It does have a certain quality, but not one you'd want to experience. Don't even think about having breakfast there. I judge hotel breakfasts by their sausages. If the sausages are good, the rest is usually OK. Maybe I hit a bad morning on my visit, because the sausages looked like the charred remains of someone's fingers, and the eggs were burnt on the bottom, uncooked on the top, and floating around in a sea of tinned tomatoes and mushrooms. Ugh! What a way to start the day.

Apart from one really good but expensive curry house, I've never found anything to like about Wolverhampton, which isn't a horseracing town. I don't like the local accent, I don't like the pubs, and there's only so much curry you can eat. I've enjoyed a couple of drinks with trainer David Evans in the racecourse bar, but, then again, who hasn't?

Although some people probably think I am a drinker bordering on being an alcoholic, I rarely have many drinks at the racecourse, with three exceptions. Three times a year I go racing with non-racing friends to Chester, York and Cheltenham. We'll drink the extortionately priced champagne at Chester and the very reasonably priced champagne at York, while at Cheltenham I rely on some of my City friends with generous expense accounts, and keep my hands firmly in my pockets. It's a day for seeing friendly faces I haven't seen for a long time and for finding out who has been made redundant and who has just received a £2 million bonus.

Cheltenham is one of my favourite racecourses but for sheer fun my top meetings are at Chester and York, with the Western Meeting at Ayr coming up fast on their heels. I come from the north, and I'm a massive fan of northern girls. They don't take themselves as seriously as southern girls do, although if you catch a train from Waterloo to Ascot and sit next to a group of hairdressers going to the royal meeting, it's like ringing a sex line, but cheaper. In the summer, on big racing days in the north, it's party time and the girls are determined to enjoy themselves. They dress up and really make a day and a night of it. In the south, I go home after racing; in the north, I've had some hilarious evenings. Some people seem to think that I always end up in bed with someone, but unless I'm completely missing something, or haven't been paying attention, I've scored a lot less times than people tell me I have. What I'm reputed to have got up to and what has actually happened are massively different, but I've certainly had some interesting times.

Chester is a terrific place, and the racetrack is an oval of pure pleasure. I look forward to their three-day May meeting more than almost any other in the calendar, and I push the boat out to stay at the Moat House Hotel, which is now the Crowne Plaza. It's expensive, but right next to the racecourse and the city centre. It was also the scene of one of my most bizarre experiences.

Readers of Viz, the adult comic, will be familiar with Buster Gonad, a character blessed (or cursed) with enormous testicles. Having often shared a room with my friend Mark 'Smudger' Smith, I was convinced that Smudger was the inspiration for Buster Gonad. If you need balls to succeed at betting, Smudger certainly had them, in abundance. One year we were joined on the train from Euston to Chester by another Mark Smith, my betting partner, and a fashionably dressed friend of his called James. Smudger got things off to a cracking start by shaking James's hand and saying, 'When I was your age, I used to wear things that made me look a c★★t as well.' As the empty Stella Artois cans piled up, so did a collection of silly bets. Finally, as we left Crewe, the subject of James's balls was raised. According to the non-Smudger Smith, they were enormous, and had been the subject of several winning bets after college football matches. Smudger and I looked at each other. We knew that, unless James suffered from some rare medical condition related to elephantiasis, our betting bank was about to get bigger. We all bet £100, Smudger and me backing Smudger's balls, and Mark and James putting their money on James.

Soon after our arrival at the Moat House, there was a knock on our door. Mark ushered in his champion, wearing a dressing gown. After several minutes of posturing and verbal sparring, James threw his dressing gown aside to reveal an admittedly impressive pair of testicles. But not impressive enough to dent our confidence. When Smudger removed the wrappings from his own collection, closer inspection wasn't required. Mark and James stood in stunned silence. 'Put your money on the table and get out,' said Smudger. 'I need some sleep.' I have had plenty of bets since then that have won me more money, but I've never backed a bigger certainty, certainly not at Chester.

Given the nature of the track, you have to accept that you will have unlucky losers, particularly if you insist on backing badly drawn hold-up horses at short prices. On the opening day of the May meeting in 2002, Kieren Fallon was riding Dragon Flyer in a five-furlong handicap. She was drawn one stall from the outside, and my gambling partner Mark Smith and I decided to sell her on the spread betting indexes. Fallon got Dragon Flyer out of the stalls quickly, crossed to the rails, and won. It should have cost us £4,500 but Mark thought that I was placing the bet and I thought that he was, with the result that the bet didn't get placed at all.

That evening, suitably grateful and looking for entertainment, I ended up outside Brannigans night club, which is a converted cinema. A sign read 'Drinking, dancing and cavorting'. Perfect. What a terrific invitation. I've accepted it several times since, and have been known to end up on the stage with a feather boa wrapped round my head. I don't know what everyone else thought, but I enjoyed it.

We've had some wild times in Chester, very much like the ones I've had in York, which is my hub for race meetings at Catterick, Ripon, Thirsk, Wetherby and Doncaster. I started staying in York for meetings at Doncaster because I couldn't find anywhere I liked in Doncaster, which is in an unenviable league of its own. The Samaritans should open a branch at the railway station because arriving there on a grey, wet Wednesday morning, which is what most mornings at Doncaster seem to be like, is enough to make anyone feel that they've had enough of life.

That's during the day. It's worse at night – a frightening time in Doncaster. Nationally, there aren't many pubs you walk into and immediately think you've made a terrible mistake, but there are in Doncaster. The atmosphere in some of them is horribly intimidating. You walk in and the pub seems to be full of huge men who look as if they'd be mining coal with their bare hands and teeth if there were any mines left in Doncaster. Since there aren't, they've been drinking since 11 a.m., been racing, lost, and are now looking at you as if you've looked at them the wrong way. They don't look like people you can reason with, and you don't want to talk to any of the women in case a nearby gorilla thinks you are making a pass at his mate.

Not that the women are very desirable. If I ever go skint, I'm going to set up a tattoo and body piercing emporium in Doncaster, because it seems to be compulsory there. The bare-midriff look is fantastic on models, but some of the women who adopt it for the St Leger meeting really shouldn't.

What finally killed Doncaster for me was getting robbed at the Regent Hotel during the Lincoln meeting in 2002. I was staying there with Dave Yates, then the Press Association's larger-than-life reporter, now the *Daily Mirror*'s larger-than-life racing correspondent. I had three grand in cash, half in my jacket pocket and half under my pillow.

We went out for another nervous evening in the town, and when we got back the money had gone. There was no sign of a forced entry, so I think it was an inside job. Earlier in the evening a smarmy barman had been wandering round asking guests if they'd be dining in the hotel, and taking room numbers. I think he was checking to see who would be going out.

Anyway, we called the police and the next morning a policeman came round. He wasn't a racing policeman, or a laughing policeman, and was amazed that I had so much cash on me. 'Don't you realise,' he said, disapprovingly, 'Doncaster's the drug and prostitution capital of the north?'

'Well,' said Dave Yates, 'we were out all night looking and we couldn't find them.'

I think my case went to the bottom of the pile after that. I certainly didn't see my £1,500 again. A couple of years later, a visiting bookmaker had a similar experience. No wonder that when I had a big win on Sixties Icon in the 2006 St Leger, it was when the race was run at York, not Doncaster.

Haydock's another disaster area. The Lancashire racecourse has got the least discerning race crowd imaginable. Hardly anyone there seems to be interested in anything but boozing, and a lot of racegoers at Newbury and Newmarket fall into the same category. If you build huge drinking halls, you have to expect huge drinking parties, which is what those racecourses get. Unless you are in the party and have drunk as much as everyone else has, it's not much fun. Newmarket's Millennium Grandstand seems to have been designed to force everyone who wants to get from the parade ring to the betting ring to walk through an army of drinkers. If you accidentally bump into a drunken gangster in a £600 suit, and spill his red wine over it, he doesn't like it, and he doesn't like you. Every time you watch a horse in the paddock and go to back it in the ring, you are taking your life into your hands. During the summer there are Friday evening concerts after racing at the July Course, which is great if you want to go to a Friday evening concert but a complete pain in the arse for anyone who is hoping to watch the horses and have a bet – me, for instance. I'm not a great fan of the town, either, and I don't stay there. I think Newmarket's dull. I've had a few wild nights at the Bedford Lodge Hotel, but even then it's been an expensive cab ride home.

No, Ayr is more like it. Through a friend, I've been lucky enough to stay at the Marine Hotel at Royal Troon, which is fantastic. There are spectacular views of the Isle of Arran and you can look out over the 18th green and imagine Tiger Woods striding up the fairway. I've had some strange and hilarious evenings there, including one which ended up with a putting competition using umbrellas and snooker cues.

One night I ended up with some friends in a night club in Troon called Pebbles. At about three a.m., the last knockings, a midget who just about reached my belly button came up to me and asked if I'd like to go to a party with her. There were various other creatures with her, and four in my group. When I looked at her lot, I wasn't surprised that no one was chatting them up, even at that desperation time in the morning. Summoning up my best Scottish drunken slur, I said, 'It's very nice of you to ask, but no thank you. I'm just going to get one more round in for the boys and then we're heading off. We've got to work in the morning.' With that, I walked over to the bar, ordered four bottles of beer, put two in each hand, and turned round to hand them out. The midget kicked me hard in the balls, screaming, 'Fuck you, then, Jimmy!' My mates roared with laughter while my knees buckled and I sank, groaning, to the floor, along with the beer. It's bad enough getting slapped for making a pass at a girl, but it's worse getting kicked in the balls for saying no thank you.

I was a bit more successful on the social front at Goodwood, although not in the company of the Earl of March. I've never been invited to stay at Goodwood House, but I have stayed at the Royal Hotel in Bognor Regis.

I don't know what King George V did for entertainment when he visited Bognor, but after one particularly long evening's drinking there, I left a pub in the company of a real two a.m. goddess. To be fair, I wasn't top of the pops either, but she looked like an overweight Karl Malden. While I was tottering back to the Royal, she suggested that I go back with her to Butlins holiday camp, where she was staying with an assortment of Tote ladies and back-row bookmakers. While we searched for a taxi, we passed the landlady of the pub we'd been drinking at. She was leaning over the bonnet of a car, with a man leaning over her with his trousers down. It wasn't a pretty sight, but they seemed to be happy. The landlady gave us a cheery wave and shouted, 'Goodnight, see you tomorrow.' I wonder if Bognor was like that in King George V's day.

By the time we got to Butlins it was about four a.m. but there was a party still going on in my paramour's chalet. Drink is a terrible thing, and seven or eight people, all out of their trees, were spread across various beds in un-romantic poses.

It must have been seven a.m. when I finally got to sleep, and when I woke up there were stinking, comatose bodies all around me. I thought, has it really come to this? I tried to open the door to the kitchen but it was blocked by beds, as were all the other doorways. The only way out was through a window. Unfortunately, we were on the first floor. I stood on the window ledge and pictured Bruce Willis in *Die Hard 2,* jumping from the wing of a plane several hundred feet above the ground, landing in some snow, and getting up. I jumped fifteen feet and didn't get up. I lay there, gasping for breath, thinking I was dying. What a way to go, found dead outside a Butlins chalet.

It was pouring with rain, I was still wearing the suit I'd worn at Goodwood the previous day, and I was soaked to the skin. When I finally staggered to the main road and found a bus stop, I felt like crying. I walked back to the Royal, dripping wet, feeling debauched and seedy. It felt as if I had hit rock bottom. But I hadn't. There was worse to come.

What I'd forgotten was that someone had been taking photographs, including one of me. I was reminded the following year when the creature from Bognor sidled up to me in a nightclub in York and asked if I'd like to buy a photograph.

'What photograph?'

'The one of you on the bed at Bognor.'

Sure enough, there I was, sitting stark naked on the edge of a bed, drinking tea. It wasn't compromising, but I felt myself starting to sweat.

'Do you want to give me £200 for it?' she asked.

I thought for a minute, then managed to pull myself together sufficiently to reply, 'I don't know who put you up to this, but if you or any of your mates want to come round and take pictures of me naked, drinking tea, you can take as many as you like.'

That seemed to work. She became apologetic and said it hadn't been her idea and she hadn't wanted to do it. Even so, it was a reminder of how easily, and dramatically, you can fall from your perch when racing, or even when not racing. I vowed never to drink tea at Butlins with my clothes off again.

Goodwood holds other unhappy memories, revolving, perhaps appropriately, around My Best Valentine. In 1997, early in July, My Best Valentine won a sprint handicap at Sandown impressively under 10st. I promptly backed it for the Stewards' Cup, at Goodwood, at about 10-1. A couple of weeks later there was a race in which I picked out a horse which came out well in John Whitley's figures, and was 33-

1. Unfortunately, it wasn't just my selection, it was also Pricewise's, in the *Racing Post*. Inevitably I struggled to get the 33-1, but, by slightly disguising the bet by putting it in a double with My Best Valentine for the Stewards' Cup, I managed to get, I think, £120 on at 33-1. When the horse won, at a much shorter price, I was in a terrific position for the Stewards' Cup.

On the day, 2 August 1997, My Best Valentine was the 9-1 third favourite. He was a hold-up horse, and jockey Ray Cochrane was a master at riding hold-up races. The 30-runner field divided into two. Drawn 23, and racing in the far-side group, Cochrane rode the perfect race, weaving through the field to put his mount's head in front on the line. Cochrane waved his whip in triumph, and the racecourse and radio commentators called My Best Valentine the winner.

But Cochrane, understandably, hadn't seen Pat Eddery and Danetime, the 5-1 favourite, on the stands side of the track. It was a photo-finish. When the result was announced, after what seemed an eternity, it revealed, as I knew it would, that Danetime had won by a neck. It was good news for Michael Tabor, Danetime's wealthy part-owner, who won over £200,000 in winning bets, but it was bad news for Dave Nevison, who stood to win about £40,000 but didn't. I needed the money rather more than Tabor.

I stood rooted to the spot where I had watched the race, on the lawn opposite the winning post, stunned. Later, when Cochrane was working for the BBC, I regularly reminded him of the day he cost me a fortune. I think there was more to be got out of My Best Valentine, and I think Cochrane had written off the small group on the stand side, and thought he'd ridden a perfect race. He had, almost.

After a decent interval – six years – not so Glorious Goodwood did it to me again. I had one of my biggest bets ever on Haripur in a seventeen-runner handicap, my sort of race, and endured the agony of watching him go clear, then get caught on the line and beaten a head by Finished Article. I was, as they say, gutted.

Bognor's got its good points, but I think Great Yarmouth, sadly misnamed, is just about the worst place in the world, with some of the ugliest women. There's definitely something about the seaside, but God knows how Great Yarmouth ever became a holiday destination. I try not to remember the hotels I've stayed in there, but can't get one out of my mind. It cost about £80 a night and, judging by the smell, was popular with the National Incontinence Society. They probably held their annual general meetings there, if not their weekly ones.

A City friend of mine had the bright idea of investing his redundancy money in a big bed and breakfast establishment in Yarmouth – God knows why. Needless to say, it ended badly. In desperation, he rented the rooms out to the Social Services department, for occupation by heroin addicts and other human disasters. After three dead bodies and a lot of hosing down, he decided enough was enough, and sold it.

The Adelphi Hotel in Liverpool is not much better. It may have been the place to stay for the Grand National at one time in the past, but not any more. Don't take my word for it. As I write this, the first ten customers' reviews of the Adelphi on the tripadvisor.com website are headed 'definitely a disappointment', 'first class dump', 'don't go', 'avoid at all costs', 'it was like being on the Titanic', 'so disappointing', 'antiquated dump', 'don't go' (again), 'are there two Adelphis in Liverpool?' and 'you might as well sleep outside', which must be some kind of record.

One year a lad who worked for Satellite Information Services and had always wanted to go to the Grand National got some vouchers from a magazine for a bargain break for two at the Adelphi. When he announced that he was going to take his girlfriend, a few eyebrows were raised, because it isn't a natural spot to take your girlfriend during Grand National week, not if you like her and are hoping to continue the relationship. Grand National week is bonus week for Liverpool's working girls, and they more or less set up their headquarters at the Adelphi. Sure enough, the lad and his girlfriend were in their room when a card appeared under the door, offering special services. His girlfriend didn't pack her bags on the spot, but after she'd spent the night thinking about the company her beloved might be keeping on trips to the racecourse, breakfast was distinctly frosty, and special services were off the menu.

It's all pretty rough as well as fairly ready in Liverpool. The year Hallo Dandy won the National, 1984, a friend and I were leaning against the bar in Yates's Wine Lodge when two ladies introduced themselves. I asked what they'd like to drink.

'We'll have two wine screamers, please.'

'I'm sorry, darling,' I said, 'I'm not from round here. What's a wine screamer?'

It was half a pint of white wine with half a pint of strong cider on top.

We slipped away as soon as possible, but at the end of the evening, in another bar, we bumped into the same two ladies. I don't know how many wine screamers they'd had but they were busy throwing ashtrays into the air then heading them. It made you think twice about a romantic night out on Merseyside.

Several years later, I tried to persuade a friend to abandon some awful blonde creature in Liverpool and bring the evening to a reasonably civilised conclusion, but I couldn't sway him, even when I told him that his new love was definitely over 60. He was adamant that she was under 40, and in the end we had a spread bet, with the mid-point 45. The next morning, he rang from somewhere in Bootle. All he said was, 'Ten, yours.'

Sex never seems to be very far away from racecourses, even at Cartmel, the popular, picturesque course near Lake Windermere. It gets so crowded there that it's a place for a day out rather than for punting, and although I like it, they are so used to ripping off tourists in the Lake District that, unless you pay through the nose, it's difficult to find somewhere cheery to stay. Perhaps my view is jaundiced by the bacon and sex. That's because I once ended up in a hotel where I was kept awake for hours by what must have been a sponsored shagathon in the bedroom above. I kept standing on the bed and giving them a round of applause, but it didn't stop her squealing and him grunting all night. At breakfast the next morning I was looking out for a couple with bags under their eyes to match the ones I'd brought down with me, but I couldn't spot them. At least two of the three of us had finally got some sleep. Then there was the bacon. It was awful.

On my travels, I've eaten much better than that, for little money. Near Leicester railway station there's a row of curry houses, all competing to offer the cheapest lunch in town. It's probably the same with the local massage parlours, because one of them is above one of the curry houses. I've never tried the massage parlour, although I've been tempted a couple of times, but I'm a regular in one of the curry houses. I may not be the most discerning of customers, but to me the food seems fantastic, and you can have as much as you can eat for £6.95. The thing to do is not to eat anything on the journey from St Pancras, then take full advantage.

If you prefer fish and chips, Catterick and Brighton are the places to go. I have a theory about fish and chip shops. It's a bad omen if there's a great big sign outside the shop claiming that they sell the best fish and chips in town. The chippie in Catterick has a nice, small, modest white sign outside, with a picture of a red fish on it. Inside, a man and his wife, both in splattered overalls, serve mushy peas. That's how it should be. In Brighton, there's a terrific shop in Woodingdean, with a sign featuring a big fisherman in a yellow oilskin jacket.

The other spot for what I think of as real food is the airport café near Folkestone racecourse. It's a truckers' café and does a fantastic all-day breakfast for about £2.50. The microwave goes 'ping', and you know your breakfast is ready. It's not haute cuisine but it's proper home cooking, eaten by men who do real work, plus a few racegoers, like me, whom the regulars look down their noses at.

Although I've had some great times stuck in racecourse bars, I'm not a great drinker at the track, except when I've had a winner as an owner, which usually means at Folkestone, Southwell, Wolverhampton or Lingfield. However, I do know some bars near racecourses quite well, including Hogans near Darlington station, a port of call on the way to, or from, Sedgefield. Hogans used to pride itself on selling the cheapest pint of bitter in the country – a claim that wasn't lost on all the alcoholics and vagrants within staggering distance, which seemed to be a huge number. I have been in there just after 11 a.m. and seen it already full of people who were barely coherent; either that or it was the local dialect. I don't know when they'd started drinking, but they'd certainly had a few by the time I arrived. Some of them looked as if they'd started twenty years ago and barely stopped since.

There are some nice pubs in the market square at Towcester, and when I go to Fontwell I always look forward to visiting the Murrell Arms at nearby Barnham. They do a lovely, huge ham hock there for about £2.95. It sets you up for the day and makes you wonder why racecourses can't do the same. I like the Benign Bishop Bar at Kelso, too, with its big roaring fire, which would be useful at Hexham, the coldest place in the world in winter.

Hamilton's a nice Scottish track. I've had some great

times there. I once went on my own and decided to have a look around Glasgow, and ended up at a nightclub called Cleopatra's Dancing Emporium. It sounded interesting, but I should have known I'd made a bad choice when my shoes kept sticking to the stairs on the way in. I ended up taking a girl to One Devonshire Gardens, an upmarket hotel with a restaurant run by Gordon Ramsay. They've got lovely palatial rooms, and it's ideal for a bit of off-the-peg philandering. Unfortunately, I discovered that my dancing companion was married to a Scottish gangster, which didn't fill me with glee. The bath was as big as most double beds, and when she jumped out of it, she slipped, fell over, and hit her head on the marble floor. I thought she was dead. I stood there and thought, I'm married, but she's married to someone who kills people for a living, and now she's dead in my bathroom. I'm going to be dead soon, too. I didn't know what to do. Luckily, she came round, but I haven't stayed at One Devonshire Gardens since, or been to Cleopatra's Dancing Emporium.

It might be safer to play games like that further from home, but I've never really been a fan of overseas racing, not even racing in Ireland. It feels as if I'm going to work but am not really at work, because I can't price the races up and am therefore never going to have any proper bets. I have been to the Breeders' Cup once, in 2005, when it was at Belmont Park, in New York. There was no more atmosphere there than at Wolverhampton on a Saturday night. I had more fun taking my two boys on a helicopter ride and up the Empire State Building than I did at the racetrack. Evidently other

Breeders' Cups have been much more exciting, and I wouldn't be against going again, although I'd prefer Chester, and Brannigans.

CHAPTER FIVE

TIPPING, BACKING AND CLAIMING

Peter 'The Lumper' has gone. A lot of the old professional racecourse punters have, which is sad. Racecourses are losing their characters. The fun used to start before you got to the course, on the train. One regular racegoer I knew, a man with plenty of money, had an obsession about avoiding paying the fare. For him, it seemed to have become the main purpose of the journey. He'd go to extraordinary lengths to avoid paying, usually spending most of his time in the toilet. If he had channelled as much energy into his punting as he did into fare-dodging, he'd have brought Ladbrokes to their knees.

The Lumper's not dead, as far as I know; he's just not at Sandown's evening meetings any more. In July, with the sun shining, he'd always be there, in a big puffa jacket stuffed with readies, hiding until his race arrived, the race he was waiting for. The Lumper's whole life was in that jacket, thousands of pounds sitting waiting for the shortest-priced favourite of the day. The shorter the price, the more the Lumper liked it, and the more he lumped on. Studying form wasn't a time-consuming exercise for the Lumper. He just went through every horse race and every dog race, looking for the shortest-priced favourite he could find. If the *Racing Post* predicted that the favourite would be 5-1 on, and when the Lumper looked along the bookmakers' boards it was 8-1 on, it seemed to make him feel better about backing it, as if it meant that the horse's chance of winning had improved. It was a staggering approach to betting. The bookies would watch him as he walked down the line. If one went 15-2 on when the rest were 8-1 on, he'd put his hand inside his jacket, pluck out £15,000 in banknotes, and put it all on, to win £2,000.

When the Lumper lumped on, the bookmakers didn't count the money, they weighed it.

He couldn't bear to watch the race itself , but if the horse won, and they usually did, his puffa jacket was a bit bigger when he left than when he'd arrived, although it was pretty big to start with. Still, I've seen him after one of his long odds-on shots has been beaten, and he's looked totally drained, standing in absolute unbelieving silence. Every bet must have taken months off his life. I think it almost sent him mad. Watching a novice chase would have been excruciating for him, which was why he tried not to watch. It was a system similar to voluntarily walking the plank: two wrong steps in a row and you drown. Maybe he's betting on Betfair now, because the commission rate is low for big odds-on punters, or maybe he's bowed out, defeated, his puffa jacket worn out. Whatever the reason, the Lumper's not seen at racecourses any more.

Paul 'The Cab Driver' is. I call him a burglar, because his approach is to 'steal' money. He used to arbitrage between the odds in the racecourse betting ring and the odds on Betfair, so he'd lay a horse in the ring at 7-4, then back it on Betfair at 2-1. Those differences don't exist any more, but the Cab Driver still backs horses in running on Betfair.

I'll be standing watching a race and suddenly hear Paul scream into his mobile phone, telling someone to back or lay a horse. He relies on the slight delay between the live action and broadcast television pictures. After a horse has safely jumped the last fence, and looks certain to win, he'll put his life on it at tiny odds, which is all right until the leader crashes through the rails, or breaks down. Sometimes the Cab Driver will try to lay a horse just as it's falling, in mid-air, which seems like an act of betting desperation to me. When a bet loses, his face looks like thunder. As a way of making money, I don't recommend it. Life's too short.

Terry 'The Juggler' is another racecourse curiosity. We used to have bets on what colour his hair would be when he turned up, blue or pink. He claimed to have been a successful art dealer before becoming the longest surviving professional punter in the game (his description), but I don't remember him ever backing a winner. He didn't seem to have a modus operandi, unless you call backing the one you fancy, then going on the chase if it loses, a system. Maybe that's why he appears on the racecourse less and less. I shouldn't think he can get the readies together.

Simon 'Dodger' McCartney always could. He was the real deal. Dodger wasn't interested in Flat racing, but he knew the jumps form inside out and had sound opinions which a lot of trainers respected. They liked him partly because, instead of asking for the trainer's opinion, which is what punters usually do, Dodger would give them his, and he was amusing company. At his peak he owned a Ferrari, an E-type Jaguar, a flat in Hampstead and a house in Epping Forest, but he went through some serious lean spells, and sometimes mixed punting with selling sunblinds and second-hand cars. Dodger must have suffered from a lack of confidence in his own ability, because he wasn't good at sticking to his guns. He would study the form, make his selections, then change his mind and back a different horse because of something a trainer or jockey had told him. I'm sure he'd have done much better backing his own judgement.

In 2002, when he was in his late sixties, Dodger was back on the racecourse after recovering from throat cancer, only to be killed in a car accident on the way from Stratford racecourse to Wolverhampton. Gay Kindersley, the former trainer and champion amateur rider, wrote an ode in McCartney's memory, and, uniquely for a professional punter, the guests at his funeral included trainers and jockeys such as Terry Biddlecombe, Richard Dunwoody and Kim Bailey. Nick Gaselee gave the memorial address. It was a sad end, and sadly, on a day-to-day basis, it seems there are fewer and fewer professional punters on the racecourse.

Barry 'The Judge' Court, whose greatest attribute is his enthusiasm, is still around. He used to be the golfer Justin Rose's caddie. Maybe that's why he seems to know so many high-profile people in racing. One day he'll have J. P. McManus, a leading racehorse owner and keen golfer, on his mobile phone, the next he'll be staying with Tony McCoy during Cheltenham. How he gets close to all these people is a mystery to me because, although Barry's a lovely fellow, he's got absolutely no sense of humour and is no fun at all. 'My name's Barry,' he'll tell people. 'People call me "The Judge". They call me "The Judge" because I am "The Judge".' Unfortunately, as far as I can see, he's a poor judge. Barry keeps a notebook with all the things he's seen in it, and he has some reasonable ideas, but I don't think he actually makes them pay.

I do have one fond memory of him. In my experience, the Ebor meeting at York in August is always a difficult one to make money at, and in 2003 I had a disastrous opening day. The next day, which was Ebor day, I backed Saint Alebe for the big race, at 20-1. On my way to the parade ring, I bumped into Barry, who told me that Saint Alebe looked magnificent, which he did. The stalls opened, and Saint Alebe stumbled out of them and tottered around for a bit while the other 21 runners got on with the business of trying to win the Tote Ebor – something traditionally impossible to do from as far behind the pace as Saint Alebe soon was. In disgust, I stopped looking and was already adding Saint Alebe to the growing list of the week's losers when I heard the horse's name mentioned in excited tones. Still last with three furlongs to run, Richard Quinn had suddenly brought Saint Alebe down the outside to take it up in the final furlong, and save the week. Barry got that one right, at least.

Maybe there are some other professional punters still on the racecourse who keep themselves to themselves, but a lot more are sat at home in front of a computer, betting on Betfair. In some ways I'd love to be one of them, but, as you'll see later, I tried it, and it was a disaster.

So I have to put up with Barry Dennis, Britain's loudest and best-known racecourse bookmaker, thanks to his appearances on Channel 4 Racing with John McCririck. Those appearances must have helped Dennis's business enormously. Punters gather round his pitch like bees around a honeypot. There are punters who want to bet with him because they've seen him on the telly, and punters who want to try to shut him up by backing a winner with him. Barry's got them all, and I certainly wouldn't want to have a pitch next to him. It's impossible to be heard over a deafening foghorn. The neighbouring bookmakers are almost redundant. Their prices are just the same, but it's Barry Dennis punters want to bet with.

I have a good relationship with Barry, and he will lay a decent-sized bet, but he is a bully who loves to abuse you. I remember one October day at Windsor in 2000. It was raining and miserable, and coming to the last two races I was about the only serious punter left in the ring. The penultimate race was a 25-runner handicap. Easy. I had £100 with Dennis on Square Dancer, at 25-1. Square Dancer won by a head, at an SP of 20-1. Barry wasn't amused. The final race was a 24-runner handicap. Even easier. I had another £100 with Dennis, this time on Chorus, also at 25-1, and Chorus won by a neck, also at an SP of 20-1. Dennis probably took about £400 on each race, and paid out £2,500 on each, all of it to me. That brought the afternoon's entertainment to an end – a very satisfactory one for me, much less satisfactory for Barry.

I think Dennis hates punters. He thinks they are all sad losers who deserve to have their money taken away from them, and he can't stand the fact that occasionally it's his money that is taken away. At that time I was betting in readies, and when I went up to collect my winnings, Barry started barking like a dog, then pretending to be sick, with all the accompanying noises, not to mention the swear words. He deliberately counted the money out painfully slowly, note by note. It wasn't the act of a gentleman, but at least he did count it out, which was the important thing.

★

By that October day in 2000 when Barry Dennis was being sick, I was tipping horses again as well as backing them, first as the 'Morning Mole' for the *Racing & Football Outlook*, then for a new weekly publication, *Raceform On Saturday,* which was launched in July 1998. My very first tip, Saskia's Hero at Market Rasen, won at an SP of 16-1, and the paper's launch coincided with my discovery of Dandy Nicholls and his skill with sprint handicappers, such as Sihafi, Double Oscar and Proud Native. Nicholls was very good at taking other people's cast-offs and improving them. That fact hadn't quite been factored into their prices yet, and it helped give me a cracking start as a tipster.

At that time, the best-known telephone tipping service in the country was The Winning Line. The Winning Line was founded in 1992 by Stephen Winstanley, a former soccer reporter who knew several keen gamblers in the Manchester United team and had known Alex Bird, a legendary professional punter from a previous era. Those contacts aroused Winstanley's interest in betting on horseracing, and The Winning Line was particularly good at attracting publicity.

After it had been been going for a couple of years, Winstanley paid Patrick Veitch a £100,000 signing-on fee as a tipster, which was unheard of. Veitch was a successful professional gambler who had run his own tipping service, called The Professional.

The relationship between The Winning Line and Veitch was short-lived, but The Winning Line branched out into racehorse ownership, with some spectacular successes. In 1998, Stretarez won the Ormonde Stakes at Chester for them, then Teeton Mill won both the Hennessy Cognac Gold Cup at Newbury and the King George VI Chase at Kempton, all in The Winning Line's colours. The following month, The Winning Line won the Peter Marsh Chase at Haydock with General Wolfe.

It was during my dizzy spell of tipping success and their dizzy spell of racing success that I was approached to join them, as The Winning Line's new tipster. I'd heard that they were meticulous and pretty ruthless, but paid well, so I finally agreed to a meeting at their offices at Alderley Edge, in Cheshire.

I was picked up from the railway station in a brand-new Mercedes and taken to their small but plush offices where, among other things, we discussed how much they were going to pay me. I was used to big sums of money from my City days, and was thinking in terms of £20,000 or £30,000 up front, then maybe £3,000 a month – terms most people would consider extremely generous. They offered me a £100,000 signing-on fee and about £10,000 a month, with a three-year contract. It seemed to me that they were offering me over £100,000 a year to record a three-minute message every day. I was staggered by the amount, but I didn't go weak at the knees. I told them I'd get someone to look at it, but I signed the deal. They said they'd make sure the £100,000 was in my account when I got home, and, true to their word, it was.

It was fantastic, but there were two problems. First, they liked the fact that I had a profile in the racing world and was seen out and about at the racecourse, but clearly thought the deal meant that I would be totally devoted to The Winning Line, which caused difficulties when it came to recording the daily messages, as you'll see. The second problem was that, as far as I could tell, the sums didn't add up, and never would. The Winning Line charged subscribers far more than other tipping services, on the basis that if something is expensive it gives it perceived additional value, a bit like expensive perfume. But you simply can't extract the sort of money they were paying me from a tipping line, even one as high profile and well run as theirs.

Before our meeting I had been spewing out winners, but when we went to lunch that day I warned them that, although I was a lot better than the average tipster, the golden period of long-priced winners wasn't going to last for ever. If I was always that successful, I'd have retired. I think they thought I was being falsely modest. They soon learnt the truth.

To supply my daily tips, I had to dial a number at a particular time, enter a code, record my message, listen to it, and re-record it if it needed changing. The message had to be recorded at 11 a.m. If it could have been done at any time up to 11, I'd have been all right, but it had to be at precisely 11 a.m. At precisely 11 a.m I was often on my way to a race meeting. So I recorded messages in coffee bars, station cafés, on high streets and on moving trains. I'd be halfway through the recording and the train might enter a tunnel, so I'd have to start again. I'd be just about to have another go when the phone would ring. It would be The Winning Line, telling me that my message should have been received, but hadn't been. 'Well,' I'd say, pretty hacked off about it, 'if you weren't on the phone, I'd be able to do the fucking message.' Subscribers would phone in and, at a crucial point during the message, hear an express train rumble by, and miss the name of my selection. They'd then phone The Winning Line to complain, and The Winning Line would phone me to chew my tender parts off, again. It just didn't work.

The Winning Line, understandably, didn't like the fact that I was messing up their messages, nor that I wasn't waiting long enough before giving my tips. I was forever being told, 'You've got to ride a finish on the horse. You can't just give them the tips. You've got to give it some build-up, and give the tips at the end of your message.' The trouble was, that just wasn't me. Besides, if you don't really want to do what you are doing, even three minutes can seem a very long time.

At one point Lester Piggott was recruited to lend his name to The Winning Line's service, and to give two or three tips a week. He was supposed to ring me at home, but getting anything out of him was like pulling teeth. I'd find myself telling subscribers, 'Lester's rung this morning and says this one will win.' Sure enough, in it went, at 13-8 on. It was the sort of tipping that was completely alien to my approach.

One day in July 1999 Lester phoned early, at 8.30 a.m. 'I've got a five-star bet for you,' he said. 'You've got to get it on the Line.' It was in a four-horse race at Yarmouth, for maiden three-year-olds. Two of them were trained by William Haggas, Lester's son-in-law. According to Lester, John Gosden's Manchuria was a certainty. As it happened, I was going to Yarmouth, so on the way I phoned in with my message. 'Lester's been on. He's never rung me like this before . . .' And so on.

I got stuck behind some lorries and just got there in time to see Manchuria, who went off at 7-4 on, being beaten easily by Westender, one of Haggas's, at 16-1. It wasn't an enjoyable sight. I walked over to the winner's enclosure, not feeling very good and about to feel worse. There was Lester Piggott, receiving the trophy, wearing the biggest grin I've ever seen on his face in my life. 'I didn't know it was that good,' he told me. He'd absolutely turned us over, and Winning Line punters had done their bollocks on an odds-on shot. Lester was totally unruffled by it. He felt no guilt at all. The only consolation was that it meant that I'd got my own Lester Piggott story, and could share it with all the other people who've got their own stories. There are two I particularly like, the one about the ice-cream, and the one about the ashtrays.

Years ago, a racing journalist who lived not far from Brighton was ghosting a newspaper column that appeared under Lester Piggott's name. Every week he had to talk to Lester to get material for the column. As you can imagine (I certainly can), it was hard work.

One week, the journalist's day off coincided with a race meeting at Brighton. He thought he'd drive the few miles to the track and enjoy a relaxing summer afternoon in the fresh air. After racing, as he was walking back to his car, he heard a familiar voice behind him. It was Lester.

'Are you going to London?' Lester asked.

'No, Lester, I'm afraid I'm not. I only live a few miles away. I'm going home.'

'That's a pity,' said Lester. 'Only I could give you some good stuff for the column.'

Reluctant, but anxious to hear what Lester had to say, the journalist agreed to drive Piggott to London, which was quite a sacrifice. As he prepared to turn right on to the London road, Lester intervened.

'No, not that way, go that way,' he said, pointing straight ahead.

'But this is the London road.'

'I know. Go that way. There's a shop I want to go to.'

Exasperated but resigned, the long-suffering journalist followed Lester's directions until eventually he was told to pull over. Lester got out, crossed the road and went into a small corner shop. A few minutes later he reappeared and got back into the car, clutching an ice-cream. He started to lick it.

'The best ice-cream in the country, this,' said Lester.

It was too much for the journalist. 'You didn't think to ask if I wanted one?' he said, sharply.

'Oh,' said Lester, looking surprised. 'I didn't know you liked ice-cream.'

It's a true story, and so is the one about the Brazilian ashtrays. In 1973, Lester phoned trainer Ron Vibert and asked if he could ride Pirate Way at Nottingham. According to

Lester, Pirate Way had been ridden the wrong way on its previous outing, and he told Vibert that if he rode the horse, it would win. Robert Ellis, the horse's owner, was in Brazil on business. He didn't normally allow his horses to run when he was away, but it had always been his ambition to have Lester Piggott ride a winner for him, so he agreed to let Pirate Way run. Pirate Way duly won, at 7-1, and to show his appreciation, Ellis brought back an expensive set of carved stone ashtrays from Brazil, which he presented to Lester at Windsor a few days later. Lester, a noted cigar smoker, looked at the ashtrays but said nothing. Ellis asked if he liked them. There was a pause.

'Can I have a cheque?' said Lester.

Yes, that's Lester Piggott.

One of the things I didn't like about The Winning Line, and don't like about tipping services generally, is the way they claim profits based on prices most of their subscribers won't have been able to get, certainly not for significant amounts. I don't feel comfortable with a service that claims to have tipped a 12-1 winner when the SP was 7-1 and very few people in the country will have got better than 9-1. I think it's better to base your results on starting prices. The claimed profit will be smaller, but I still think it's a good marketing ploy.

On the other hand, I think all tipping services are doomed to failure in the long run, because markets are self-regulating, the betting market more than any other, and they quickly adjust to accommodate a successful tipping line. The bad tipping services fail of their own accord, because their results aren't good enough and the marketing costs eat up any profits they make from premium-rate telephone calls. The good ones eventually struggle because, if they are good, they attract a lot of new clients, there is a lot of money going on to their selections, and bookmakers act to push down the prices. The service can no longer make worthwhile profits for its clients, who are paying a lot for this top outfit's advice, and subscribers eventually start looking at the next new service that is doing well.

My tips for The Winning Line did pretty well. I was in profit most months, but after about eight months the relationship started to go a bit sour. If I put up a couple of losers in a row, Winstanley would suddenly ring me at home and tell me that he fancied a particular horse. Did this mean I was supposed to tip the horse he fancied? He and his partner, Nigel Stewart, were nice chaps but aggressive, in-your-face marketing men. Winstanley had had a heart and lung transplant a few years earlier and suffered from serious mood swings, I think from the drugs he had to take, which made him difficult to deal with; but I think the main problem was that, despite introducing new premium-rate services, The Winning Line didn't bring in enough money to justify the cost of employing me.

One day I rang in and said, 'Everything OK?'

'Well, no, Dave, actually it isn't. We're not doing this any more.'

'I think you are,' I said, 'because I've got a document here that says you've got another 24 months to go.'

I went to a solicitor to see where I stood, and we sent a letter about breach of contract, because as far as I was concerned I hadn't done anything wrong and had abided by the terms of the contract. But they could probably have closed the business down and given me nothing. In the end, Nigel and I met at Wolverhampton, agreed on three months' money and shook hands.

Really, we are on different sides of the game. Nigel Stewart and Stephen Winstanley were clever men, and I'm sure they prospered subsequently, but I wasn't right for The Winning Line, nor it for me. Sadly, Winstanley died in 2007.

There is a huge difference between tipping horses and backing them. The winner I have tipped that ends up at 3-1 may have been 4-1 on my tissue and 5-1 in newspaper betting forecasts. Although my tissue isn't cast in stone, I would probably not have backed the horse myself if 3-1 was the best price available in the ring. In fact, I might well have ended up backing something else instead, a horse that turned out to be available at a significantly longer price than in my tissue. It's frustrating to watch a horse I've tipped win, and still lose money, and it's even worse when the horse I've tipped loses, and I am seen in the stands cheering home the 16-1 winner.

Both those scenarios have happened to me several times, because my betting is driven by prices rather than selections. When I do guest spots on Racing UK, some of the presenters want me to give tips and others just want my view of the race. If I give a tip, I tend to say, this is the most likely winner and I think it's worth backing if it's at least, say, 9-4. If I'm asked for a tip in the street, or at the racecourse, I always give the favourite, because it shortens the conversation and is generally what people want to hear. They don't want to hear the truth, which is that everything depends on the price.

Now that my newspaper and television work has made me a more widely recognised figure at the racecourse, people frequently come up to me, wanting to pick my brain, which can be irritating. I'm a pretty affable and approachable person but if someone keeps sidling up to me at the racecourse asking what I think, and they happen to catch me at the wrong moment, perhaps after I've just done my bollocks on a race, I can get nasty. I've got a fairly long fuse, but I have called several people four-letter names and told them never to come up to me again.

One racecourse regular who was always pumping me for information came up to me one day at Sandown in July 2002 and asked about John Best's two runners in a maiden auction race for two-year-olds. When I didn't show any enthusiasm for discussing them with him, he complained, 'If you'd got Aids you wouldn't give it to me.' He was right. Not if I thought about what it would involve. After the outsider of Best's two runners, Desert Spirit, won at 33-1, the nuisance turned up again to ask if I'd backed it. I told him that I hadn't, which was the truth, but judging by the number of four-letter words he used beginning with either an f or a c, I don't think he believed me.

★

My dubious contribution to The Winning Line was soon followed by an even more dubious contribution to talkSPORT radio. During the summer of 2000 I was invited to co-host a weekly phone-in on racing with Ian Carnaby, a well-known sports broadcaster and racing journalist. We'd turn up at the studio every Sunday morning so that anyone who had done their money the previous day could try to make themselves feel a bit better by picking up their phone and venting their frustrations on us for an hour.

There were several problems, the biggest being that there weren't enough callers, or enough listeners. Although I'd appeared on television and radio before, it had always been as someone responding to questions put by a presenter. This time I was joint presenter, on a commercial radio station, and it just wasn't me. I got bollocking after bollocking from the producer because I was supposed to keep saying, 'Keep your calls coming in,' and repeating the station's telephone number, and I kept not doing it. 'If you don't give them the number, how are people supposed to know what number to ring?' the producer would bawl at me, but I just couldn't bring myself to say it. It was a commercial operation and they were paying me to do it, but perhaps because of some odd moral objection, it stuck in my throat. I couldn't get it out. I was totally useless at it. Ian is a professional broadcaster and kept going, kept ad-libbing, while I just sat there thinking, when is this nightmare going to end?

When I did get asked a question, it was quite often from someone who knew me, trying to trip me up and have a joke at my expense. The call I remember best was from a man who had just missed out on a six-horse accumulator: the first five had won but the last one had been beaten in a photo-finish. He asked if I could give him any advice on betting strategy. I said, 'Yes: try a five-horse accumulator.'

Needless to say, the programme was short-lived. It lasted for just six episodes, and there clearly wasn't going to be a second series. The best thing about it was going to the pub with Ian afterwards, and getting to know him better. That was good fun, but I haven't been asked to host a phone-in since.

★

I gave up claiming horses for a different reason. Death threats made me lose my enthusiasm for it.

I'd been impressed by John Best, who took out a jump trainer's licence in 1997 and one for the Flat two years later. In bad all-weather races, Best's horses were among the worst, but they always looked well, and enough of them finished fourth or fifth at long prices to make me think that with better horses he might succeed. Best trained in Kent, where I lived, and I met him through Alan Turner, a racehorse owner who was helping Best get started. Best had ridden and trained point-to-pointers and hunter chasers but didn't come from a racing background and had no interest in betting. He freely admitted that he knew very little about the programme book or strategies for campaigning horses, but he was a grafter and was keen to learn.

I had bits and pieces of horses with him and, with my betting going well, in 2001 I got involved in buying yearlings for the first time, in partnership with others. We bought four horses, not with the intention of establishing Nevison Bloodstock Enterprises but to help Best get off the ground, and get new owners involved in the yard through syndication. Syndication isn't something I'd want to be deeply involved in because it takes up a lot of time in relation to the financial returns. The horses were all sold, either immediately or later on, and did quite well. In 2002, Ally Makbul, who cost 3,000 guineas, finished second on her debut, in my colours, and eventually won three times, still trained by Best, in Malcolm Ward's name. Whippasnapper, who also cost 3,000 guineas, also finished second on his debut, and on his third outing, at Windsor, won in the name of a partnership that included Ward, me and others. Whippasnapper won another two races for us, and went on to win four more for Vanessa Church, still trained by Best.

After a very financially successful 2002, I was involved again when we bought seven two-year-olds at Doncaster's 2003 breeze-up sales for a total of 125,100 guineas. All of them were eventually winners, but the first return came within a month, when a parcel arrived for me at home. Unfortunately I was away at the races, so Lotte, my wife, opened it. I hadn't told her that I'd signed for Otago, for 30,000 guineas, Little Eye, for 27,000 guineas, and Best Desert and St Savarin, for 21,000 guineas each, so she was rather surprised to read that the enclosed tie was a present from Doncaster Bloodstock Sales, in appreciation of my custom. Lotte immediately phoned me. There weren't many jokes during the conversation, but there were various references to school fees and family responsibilities. I tried to explain that it wasn't all my money, and that we'd be selling the horses on, but my plea for mitigation fell on stony ears.

By the time Lotte had finished savaging me, I was hoping that the tie would be long enough to hang myself, if I was ever allowed back in the house to knot it.

The previous year, Best and I had started to claim more horses, having claimed a few in the past. In January, at Southwell, I claimed Tweed from Malcolm Jefferson's yard for £4,000. I then sold half of Tweed to Paul Dixon, a big owner, on the understanding that the horse would run in his colours but still be trained by Best. Nine days after claiming him, Tweed won a better-class race, worth over £4,000 to the winner, at Wolverhampton. By the end of February he'd won another three races.

I wish it always worked out like that. It rarely does. That April, I claimed a horse called Collard for 7,500 guineas after she won an apprentice selling race at Wolverhampton. It wasn't my shrewdest purchase. I'd barely written out the cheque before Collard went lame. She could hardly make it to the horsebox. We managed to race her twice more, unplaced, and sold her for 5,500 guineas, which under the circumstances was a great result. She hasn't run since.

I had some decent bets on the horses we claimed, but I didn't buy them as vehicles for betting. As with our yearling purchases, they were intended to help build up Best's business. Nowadays, it is supposed to be much more acceptable to buy a horse at the auction that follows selling races, or to claim horses, than it used to be in the past, when a lot of people frowned on it. That may well be true, but if there has been a change in attitude, it certainly hasn't percolated through to everybody.

You might think that if a horse's connections enter a horse for a selling or claiming race in which one of the race conditions is that the winner and other runners are entered to be sold or claimed, the connections shouldn't be surprised, nor should they complain, if their horse is indeed sold or claimed. Unfortunately, some people still think it's a hanging offence, and are quite prepared to arrange for the hanging.

The first death threat came the year before my flurry of buying activity, in 2001. I claimed a horse and shortly afterwards received an anonymous phone call to say that, if I knew what was good for me, I would take the horse to a particular place and leave it there. Instead, I reported the incident to the police and to the Jockey Club's security department. This was followed by threats to shoot John Best's horses on his gallops.

I'm not easily intimidated, and the experience didn't stop me claiming horses, but another, even worse, experience did, and I haven't claimed a horse since.

On the second occasion, I wasn't at the race meeting myself but had arranged for a claim to be submitted on my behalf. That evening I was in my car when the carphone rang.

'Was that you who claimed that horse?'

'Yes.'

'Well, you don't know who you've claimed it from, but they're not very happy.'

I started off by adopting an aggressive stance. 'Look,' I said, 'I've had this before. I don't care who they are. If there's any funny business, I'm going straight to the police.'

The man said, 'I'm just the messenger boy, but these are serious people and I'm going to have to give them your telephone number.'

I said, 'Give them my number, I don't care,' but I was shaking as I was driving along. It wasn't a nice feeling.

Sure enough, about ten minutes later the phone rang again. It was someone else, but the subject was the same. The new caller made it abundantly clear that these people wanted the horse back; and not only did they want it back, they also wanted £2,000 in cash for the inconvenience I'd caused them. I argued a bit, and said that I certainly wasn't going to give them £2,000, but he just said, 'You ask around a bit.' So I made a few enquiries, and was told that the people I was dealing with could be particularly persuasive. Finally I approached a bookmaker who I thought might know them.

'Look,' I said, 'I might be in a spot of bother. I've claimed a horse – it's owned by so-and-so.'

The bookmaker sucked in a mouthful of air and said, 'Ooooh, if I was you I'd give the horse back.'

'I'm starting to think that might be the best policy,' I said, 'but they also want two grand on top.'

There was another pause. 'You know what, Dave? That might just be the best two grand you'll ever spend.'

Before I finally gave in, I made one last call, to a retired prizefighter who was familiar with the world inhabited by my new acquaintances. He promised to look into it for me. I was hoping he'd hurry up, because every time I went racing I kept looking at the crowd, expecting to see a marksman lining me up. Eventually I saw my boxing acquaintance.

'Dave,' he said, 'I think he wants his horse back.'

We took the horse to where we were told to take it, and they took it back, although at least I held out against paying the £2,000. Later, I got a phone call to say they appreciated what I'd done and if I ever needed anything sorting out, I just had to call them. I haven't done. I'm just hoping they don't call me.

★

I'm not too keen on hearing from the BBC again, either. The last time I heard from them was in 2002, when they were preparing a 'Kenyon Confronts' programme on skulduggery in racing.

I was at Lingfield one day when a man in his sixties with a Liverpool accent came up to me and said he and his friend wanted to buy a horse. He told me that his friend had a load of money. His friend, who was about 25, looked like Brian May, the Queen guitarist, but without the talent. The picture I was given was of a posh kid with too much money and an older man wanting to acquire some himself. They told me that they already had a bumper horse in Ireland with Willie Mullins, a top trainer. The horse was by Be My Native and was doing aeroplane times on the gallops. They wanted to move it over here and land a touch with it, and were thinking of putting it with John Best. I think they chose Best because they knew I was involved with the yard and thought it must be a gambling stable, but they'd picked the wrong people.

I said I'd talk to Best but realised that something was badly amiss when the older man told me that he'd once owned Amaranda and Ekbalko. I could hardly stop myself laughing because I knew that Amaranda, a leading two-year-old in 1977, had been owned by 'Budgie' Moller, while Ekbalko, a very good and popular hurdler in the early 1980s, had been owned by an Arab, Tawfik Fakhouri. I didn't challenge him, though. I just thought he was a bullshitter and that I'd let the nonsense run on for a bit, and see where it took us. I didn't realise it was part of a television sting. Anyway, it was agreed that they'd come to Best's yard to discuss having a horse there.

When they arrived, the Brian May lookalike soon started talking about stopping the horse they were going to bring from Ireland and then landing a touch with it. I asked him why he wanted to stop it, if the horse was putting up such good times on the gallops. Why not just enter it for a suitable race and back it to win? Well, he said, we want to have a proper touch. He kept going on about it, and when we were watching some horses working, he then started asking if there was anything you could give a horse to make it go slower or faster. 'Yes,' I said, 'if you want to go to prison.'

Eventually, when I suppose he realised he wasn't going to get anywhere with us, he asked who he should go to if he really wanted a gamble. I told him to be careful but suggested the names of a few trainers who liked to lay horses out for a touch. John and I discussed it, and I then contacted the Jockey Club to tell them what had happened. The Jockey Club subsequently sent out a letter to trainers warning them about suspicious, probably bogus owners.

We didn't know that the two men were television reporters and that they had been secretly recording and filming us, but several weeks later each of us received a letter from the BBC. Mine included quotes from our meetings, including me talking about the time when my friend Ray had been rolling around in a pile of banknotes after Teenage Scribbler had landed a gamble for us at Catterick. I didn't particularly want the conversations broadcast on television, but I hadn't said anything that wasn't true, or that I needed to feel ashamed of. John felt the same about the quotes in his letter, so we both rang the BBC and told them to go ahead and use whatever they wanted. Best went so far as to ask to appear on the programme and be interviewed. Needless to say, the BBC told us that they wouldn't be using the material. Evidently they approached seven trainers but the programme only looked at three: Ferdy Murphy, Jamie Osborne and David Wintle.

It wasn't a very pleasant experience. Nor were all my other experiences of television. I now enjoy my appearances on Racing UK, but when I first appeared on the original Attheraces programmes, it was often boring. Sometimes it involved doing three shows, all exactly the same. I'm not a natural at it, although I think I've improved quite a lot.

There were often times when I'd sit and work out how much a day's television work had cost me in missed betting opportunities. One particular afternoon, when I was working with presenter Robert Cooper, a lovely man but not a regular user of Betfair, the job certainly cost me money. I had backed a novice hurdler at Kempton with a view to laying it in running. I'd got Betfair up on my laptop screen and was watching the race, with Robert sitting in front of the computer under instructions to lay the horse when I told him to. I was thinking aloud, and told him to lay it, but didn't realise that Bob started to lay it, and kept on laying it, and laying it. The horse won, and I was smiling, thinking that I was in profit, having backed it to win more than I'd laid it to lose. I asked Bob what he'd done and he gave me a puzzled look and said, 'I don't know. The screen's gone red.' When I looked, the figure on display wasn't a profit, but a loss, quite a big one. 'That's more than I earn in a month,' said Bob. It was agony.

Trying to mix betting and television wasn't working too well, and soon after that unfortunate episode I gave up Attheraces. Later, I bumped into Jim Ramsey, who had been the channel's editor but had since joined Racing UK. He asked if I'd like to appear on their outside broadcasts and I now do two or three meetings a month, usually lesser meetings, which suits me because I will often not have had a bet. I enjoy it, and find it relaxing. I'm a lot less agitated than I used to be.

It would be easy not to say anything controversial on television, but I think I am paid to express opinions. I feel that The Morning Line on Channel 4 used to be better a few years ago, when the team were more opinionated. Now it's a back-slapping club, like daytime television for old ladies. Admittedly, if you stick your neck out with a strong opinion it does sometimes get chopped off. One Saturday in September 2006, Nick Luck and I were discussing a race at Newbury in which Godolphin had two quite fancied runners. Ten minutes earlier, at Ayr, another of Godolphin's horses, Ashaawes, had finished unplaced at odds-on. We were both saying how dangerous it was to support the stable's runners at the moment, because they seemed to be under a bit of a cloud. A couple of minutes later Godolphin had a one-two at Newbury, with Blue Ksar winning at 8-1 and Emirates Skyline second at 9-2. We looked like prize chumps, and Betfair's chatroom came alive with unflattering remarks about our judgement, or lack of it.

Still, you've got to fill the airtime with something, and I think it's more interesting to fill it with your opinions than to play safe and sit on the fence, which is what I think some television pundits are guilty of. You don't have to slag people off, but not all trainers and jockeys are terrific at training or riding horses, and even the good ones are not good all the time. I think you are duty-bound to criticise when you think it is justified.

When it comes to making predictions, Pat Murphy leaps off the fence only when the result is no longer in doubt, Willie Carson has a habit of claiming the credit for dubious goals, Peter Scudamore is naive about betting, and I've got a phobia about Simon Mapletoft, who has mastered the art of saying absolutely nothing with an awful lot of words. I can't listen to him for more than ten seconds. The same applies to Derek 'Thommo' Thompson. Lesley Graham never says anything of any interest to punters, and Alex Hammond and Zoey Bird look terrific but also never say anything of any use. It seems to me they are there merely to give viewers a change from watching middle-aged men.

Lydia Hislop is different. I think she sometimes falls into

the trap of voicing strong views for the sake of it, perhaps because she sees herself as a woman in a man's world, but I would much rather that than listen to someone who makes a point of never being controversial. I'd rather listen to someone I disagree with than to someone who either has no view or is not prepared to express it. Both Lydia and James Willoughby grate on me after a while, but at least they sometimes come up with a golden nugget.

They would be in my 'B' team. My 'A' team is led by Eddie Fremantle, to whom I owe a debt of gratitude for having shown me how to construct my own tissues, and for introducing me to an approach to betting that suits my temperament. I respected his opinion then, and I respect it now. Steve Mellish, Graham Cunningham and Jonathan Neesom are the others in my 'A' team. They are the people I listen to; the rest, I don't listen to – except for commentaries. I think, as a group, television commentators are generally good. That certainly applies to Richard Hoiles, Ian Bartlett, Stewart Machin and Simon Holt. 'Aussie' Jim McGrath's descriptive phrases have lost their freshness, Mark Johnson starts riding a finish and cranking it up to full volume four fences from home, while Graham Goode sounds as if he's not interested any more. Listening to him reminds me of Ronnie Corbett's impersonation of a golf club bore.

CHAPTER SIX

BATTLING FOR BREAD
AND BUTTER

A bread-and-butter Thursday at Chepstow. The bread will be thicker than most punters slice it, and the butter – well, that will be thicker, too. And the jam, if there is any.

By the time I've been picked up at Swindon station, I've already passed my tissue of prices to Mark Smith, my betting partner, so that he can get to work, scouting around for the best ways to exploit the discrepancies between my prices and the ones available in the marketplace. During the journey, across the toll bridge over the Severn Estuary, Mark and I exchange phone calls. 'Do a match for £50 and do a big bet on it,' I tell him.

We are talking about the three-mile novices' chase. In my tissue, I have Principe Azzurro at evens and Fast Forward at 5-2. I think Principe Azzurro is at least a stone better horse, and they are racing off level weights. The trouble is, the fences have tended to get in Principe Azzurro's way. On Betfair, Fast Forward is 13-8 and Principe Azzurro 15-8. Mark will back Principe Azzurro in a match bet with Fast Forward, and have several hundred pounds on Principe Azzurro to win.

It's a slightly odd day because I fancy the short-priced horses. I'm always looking for ways of getting favourites beaten, but you mustn't invent reasons to oppose them. Even so, experience tells me that when you support the favourites, the upside isn't usually huge.

Whoever did the betting forecast in the *Racing Post* for the opening maiden hurdle must have been drunk, because there is no way that Snow Patrol will be 11-4. Philip Hobbs's six-year-old will be favourite, but not 11-4 favourite. I wish. He's entered for the Supreme Novices' Hurdle at

Cheltenham and there's nothing else with any form in today's race. I've got Snow Patrol in my tissue at 4-5 with Man Overboard, who is 5-1 in the *Post*, at 8-1. So at 11.20 a.m. I'm on the phone to Mark again, to see what he's been doing. We're buying Snow Patrol over Man Overboard in a match bet for £100 a length, with Snow Patrol giving Man Overboard four lengths. Man Overboard has run only once before, last March, when he pulled quite hard in a bumper race. If he's wearing a cross-noseband, or looking too keen in the parade ring or on the way to the start, I may go in again. It's a fairly risky bet, because if it goes wrong we will be £1,900 down. With the ground heavy, any match bets are likely to make up to the maximum distance of fifteen lengths, which can be a good thing or a bad thing – I'll tell you later.

As well as Principe Azzurro and Snow Patrol, I think Boomshakalaka in the other division of the maiden hurdle is entitled to be a strong favourite. Mark and I discuss the details of a trixie, a bet in which three selections are combined in three doubles and a treble, and end up with three £200 win doubles and a £400 win treble, at odds of 7-4, 4-5 and 7-4. If Snow Patrol and one of the other two win, the bet is virtually covered. We've gone top heavy on the treble, so that if they all win, it should be a good winning day.

A trixie on short-priced horses isn't a favourite bet of mine. I'd rather find horses at 9-2 and 8-1 in sixteen-runner handicaps, horses I am confident will be placed, and combine them in an each-way double. If both win, it's a terrific day, and if both are placed, it's still an OK day. That isn't an option today. There's nothing that fits the bill.

The Cheltenham Festival is less than a month away, so we've been scouring the special bets on offer, and have come up with a cracker. A few bookmakers, including Paddy Power, are offering prices about the longest winning starting price at what is now a four-day meeting. You can get 11-8 against there being a winner with an SP of 40-1 or more. Mark has been doing some research. In 2004, before the Festival was extended to four days, there was a 40-1 winner, Maximize, and a 50-1 winner, Creon. The following year, when there were 24 races, Another Rum won the four-mile National Hunt Chase for amateur riders at 40-1. Last year, on good ground, Shamayoun won one handicap hurdle at 40-1 and Kadoun won another at 50-1. I don't know where they get 11-8 against from, because it's an odds-on shot in my book, especially since the going looks as if it will be at least good to soft this year and may be softer, with massive fields guaranteed. Whatever we can get on, we'll get on. So far we've had £1,200. It'll soon have been backed down to evens, but I'd be willing to back it down to about 4-6, and I expect to end up winning about £6,000.

The press room at Chepstow is like a rabbit warren, and Chepstow is not a course that does anything for me. The track itself looks lovely, but that is the best thing about it. Visiting the racecourse is no better than watching it on television. I love watching the Welsh National at Chepstow – on television. It's been changed by people with no feel for racing. They've moved the parade ring to the front of the stands, leaving the old parade ring like a wasteland, and the pre-parade ring is now hopeless. You have to stand on a hill and look down at the horses, which is no good at all. At least the bookmakers here are all right, the entire front row. If you want a bet, you can get on.

The phone rings. It's Mark. He's done the Jackpot at Kelso. It was a marginal decision because there was only a carry-forward of £16,697, building up to £36,569 by the time racing starts. Sculastic is 6-1 on in the opening novices' hurdle, and we've got it as a banker, as have most other people. Mark's also had £800 at 2-1 against Sculastic winning by less than ten lengths. Mark has been pricing them up at Kelso and, as he's got most of the favourites in at shorter prices than they are forecast to start at, we discuss whether or not to buy the favourites' index on the spreads. Another option would be to sell the starting price index, but that is dangerous. If Sculastic loses, the winner could be 200-1. In the end we do neither, and unfortunately Sculastic does lose, badly. English City wins at 33-1. That's £1,735 down the drain on the Jackpot, and another £800 because Sculastic didn't win by less than ten lengths: he didn't win at all. It's a bad start. We are over £2,500 down already and they haven't even run the first at Chepstow.

More phone calls.

'What do you think of Numero Un De Solzen?' Mark asks.

'I think he's even money.' In the *Racing Post*, Numero Un De Solzen is 9-2 for the amateur riders' chase at Kelso. 'Let's look at the match bets. It's not going to fall, is it? It hasn't so far.'

1.22 p.m. Eighteen minutes until the first at Chepstow,

Snow Patrol's race. We have £600 to win at 2.9 on Betfair and £200 at 7-4 with an off-course bookmaker. In the parade ring, Man Overboard is wearing a cross-noseband. The man walking him round is trying to keep him calm. There's nothing I don't like about the look of Snow Patrol. He looks fitter than Man Overboard, tighter, more defined.

The phone again. 'I wouldn't mind going again in this match, Snow Patrol, Man Overboard. He looks fat.' Mark buys another £50, this time giving up five lengths to Man Overboard. He also buys Snow Patrol over Nanard for £20, giving up four lengths. We need Snow Patrol to win well.

In the ring, his price is tumbling: 11-8 a few minutes ago, Snow Patrol is now odds-on and Man Overboard 8-1, and drifting. As they line up, the favourite is 8-11 and Man Overboard 11-1. My tissue was right.

Snow Patrol leads virtually the whole way and wins by five lengths from Gunnasayso with Man Overboard, who ran well, six lengths further back and Nanard a well-beaten fourth. Good. One way or another, we've got back what we lost at Kelso, and have the first leg of our trixie in place.

We put £555 on Boomshakalaka at 1.92 on Betfair in the next, and to start with I'm happy to see Back Among Friends tear off in the lead, which is what he often does. I expect him to pay for it later on, but Jim Old's eight-year-old maiden doesn't stop, and doesn't fade. He keeps going, and Boomshakalaka, who was backed down to 13-8 on, just isn't good enough to get to him on the sticky ground and is well beaten. That's ruined the trixie, not to mention the £555.

It's windy. In the parade ring, the horses for the 2.45 p.m., a juvenile maiden hurdle, are skittish. I have Darusso at 5-1 in my tissue and back him at 8.66 on Betfair. We are trying to back Stumped at 3.1 but are not going to get that price on the favourite, and I won't take less. Being by Bertolini, there must be a chance that Stumped won't stay the trip at this track, on this ground. Unfortunately, he does, backed in to 5-4, with Darusso second, at 5-1.

At Kelso, Numero Un De Solzen finishes a close-up third, never quite looking like winning. It means we've lost £600 to bookmakers and more from including him in various trixies. The good news is that we had Numero Un De Solzen in match bets with Mel In Blue, who finished more than fifteen lengths behind Numero Un De Solzen. That was worth £1,140 to us.

Even on a relatively quiet betting day like this, it's difficult to know exactly how much up or down I am at any given moment, because there are bets sitting on the exchanges which may or may not be taken up, and Mark is constantly looking for new opportunities.

Principe Azzurro's jumping didn't let him down and he went off as the 6-4 favourite, but Fast Forward got the better of him, by one and three quarter lengths. The damage on the match bets is nothing, but it's sunk more trixies. Pity.

Milan Deux Mille stands out in the next race, a handicap chase – stands out as one to oppose, that is. David Pipe's improving five-year-old has won four chases in a row, all in the space of a month. His handicap mark has gone up almost three stone, and last time, at Kempton less than a week ago, he jumped alarmingly left. Kempton is a right-handed track while Chepstow is left-handed, which should suit Milan Deux Mille, but there is a good chance that this will be one race too many for him at the moment, and Pipe may have it in mind that if Milan Deux Mille does get beaten today it will at least discourage the handicapper from putting him up still further.

I would like to oppose him in some match bets but, although he is the forecast favourite, the spread betting firms don't seem to be keen to have Milan Deux Mille in their match-ups. We end up buying Mister Quasimodo over Milan Deux Mille for £20, giving away 2.5 lengths, even though Mister Quasimodo starts at 4-1 and Milan Deux Mille at 7-2. We're not the only spread bettors wanting to oppose Pipe's horse. On the exchanges, we lay Milan Deux Mille for a place, £555 at 1.95, and back five other horses to win.

Sometimes you can be right, yet lose money. Milan Deux Mille gets beaten seventeen lengths but Mister Quasimodo is pulled up, along with No Full, one of the 7-2 co-favourites, and Milan Deux Mille ends up third of only five finishers. To add insult to injury, the winner, Nozic, was just about the only horse we didn't back! How did we manage to lose on that?

In the press room, Eddie 'The Shoe' Fremantle is watching the 4.10 p.m. at Kelso. It's a fourteen-runner 0-90 handicap chase, which makes it little better than a seller, full of horses who have a tremendous talent for not winning. Eddie and I have a £2 bet with each other; he has all the horses with even numbers running for him, and I have all the odd numbers running for me. We both get a lot more animated than if we'd had £200 on something. I've got the first and second favourites, Political Cruise and Ryminster, on my side. Lethem Present, number 8, looks to have the race won but is caught close home by Wensley Blue, number 16. There is much shouting and mocking. Eddie is doing both, with me as the victim.

No sooner is that over than there's another 0-90 handicap chase, at Chepstow. It's not my kind of race, and I let it pass. I don't feel that I've got things massively wrong today, it's just one of those days.

Not quite over yet, though. My tissue for the closing novices' hurdle reads 7-4 Pyleigh Lady, 9-2 Michael Muck, and 6-1 What A Scientist, which isn't very different from the betting forecast in the *Racing Post*. I think Pyleigh Lady is the most likely winner, and she's being backed, into 11-8. Of course there's a temptation to back her, particularly since I am down on the day, and this is the last race, but not giving in to the temptation is one of the things that sets me apart from most other punters. If I back Pyleigh Lady at 11-8 when she's 7-4 in my tissue, then I'm throwing the system I rely on to make a living out of the window. And it isn't the last race, although a lot of punters will be betting as if it is. I suspect that bookmakers in the ring will take twice as much on this race as they did on the first. Why? Because punters who have made a profit during the afternoon will be playing up their winnings, while punters who are down will be trying to recover their losses. But there's no such thing as a last race, at least not until you give up or keel over. There's always tomorrow.

I don't feel that Pyleigh Lady is a good favourite to oppose, but I'm going to oppose her by backing two horses I don't think will win, which will seem stupid to many punters, and feels strange to me. Why am I doing it? Not out of desperation or mental illness but because on Betfair I can get almost 7-1 against Michael Muck, which is over 50 per cent better than on my tissue, and I can get over 11-1 against What A Scientist, which is over 80 per cent better than on my tissue. I have to back them. I have £444 on Michael Muck and £222 on What A Scientist.

Pyleigh Lady ends up at evens but, with Tony McCoy riding as only he can on What A Scientist, Darren O'Dwyer's mount just fails to pin him back. It's a great result for us and eats a decent hole in the day's losses, but when everything is totted up – the exchange bets, the spread bets, the fixed-odds bets – the final figure is still minus £2,388. Don't ever think it's easy.

CHAPTER SEVEN

POOLS, SPREADS AND EXCHANGES

The Tote was founded in 1928, Sporting Index in 1992, and Betfair in 1999. One way or another, they have all shaped my life as a professional punter, and Betfair has changed every British punter's betting world.

During Royal Ascot, before they knocked the grandstand down and built another one, I used to go to the viewing area reserved for the press, at the top of the stand, and park myself next to the Tote screens. The Tote facility there wasn't used much, and it was a good spot to monitor the Tote's prices. The Tote has a different clientele from the bookmakers, particularly at the big meetings - the Cheltenham Festival, Aintree's Grand National meeting, the Guineas meeting at Newmarket, the May meetings at Chester and York, the Epsom Derby, Goodwood week, York's Ebor meeting, St Leger week at Doncaster, and Royal Ascot in June - where there are a lot of once-a-year punters with no conception of value. They will take 7-2 about a 7-1 chance because Frankie Dettori is riding it, and many of them prefer to bet with the Tote, because the Tote ladies are less intimidating than the ring bookmakers. If money pours through the Tote windows on to Frankie's mount, the odds against other runners are pushed out, and some of the prices represent good value.

There was a time when, if the win pool topped £100,000, which it did for every race at Royal Ascot, I would look at the prices on my tissue and compare them with the Tote prices as well as with the prices in the betting ring. If the Tote odds were the longest for a particular horse, then I backed it with the Tote. Because the pools were strong, you could have a reasonable size bet without it affecting the horse's price too much. If I'd priced a horse up at 16-1 on my tissue, and it was showing 27-1 on the Tote, I could back it to win £5,000 and the Tote dividend would still pay about 22-1.

That was before the rise of internet betting and betting exchanges. Their arrival meant that people could sit at home and arbitrage between fixed-odds prices and Tote prices, so it was no longer worth my while to stand in front of the Tote screens at Royal Ascot. Nowadays, the vast majority of the Tote bets I have are on the Tote Jackpot and the Scoop6. They appeal to me partly because they offer the chance of big wins, which are the kind of wins I want, but also because a lot of clever gamblers don't get involved in Jackpot bets, concentrating instead on the betting exchanges and fixed-odds betting. To a considerable extent, when I have a Jackpot or Scoop6 bet, I am betting against the general betting public, which gives me an edge.

Of course, the big professional syndicates step in when the Jackpot or Scoop6 pool hasn't been won for a while, and there is a big rollover, but I will have a go when the pool is smaller than it probably has to be for the syndicates to become involved. If there is £30,000 in the Jackpot pool, I may play, as long as it looks 'gettable' and there is at least one vulnerable favourite on the card. When the pool reaches £50,000 I will usually be involved, unless the Tote do what they sometimes do when they don't want the Jackpot to be won that day, and choose a meeting with an impossible card. On that kind of card, where every favourite might be 5-1, a £1 accumulator would win at least £46,000, even if the favourites won every race, which doesn't make the Jackpot very appealing. My rule of thumb is that if you multiply the expected odds of the horses you have made favourite by £1, and the figure is close to the amount in the pool, you shouldn't play.

Another deterrent is the high cost of increasing the size of your permutation of selections. You can easily end up with a perm that is going to cost you £8,000. Do you really want to risk that on your selections?

Doing the Jackpot usually means producing a list of horses that has to be trimmed down, one way or another. There are all sorts of ways of doing it, including making some selections bankers, but you always have to be thinking, if I put in this amount of money, how much am I likely to win? There is not much point putting in £5,000 if you don't expect to win more than £6,000. In my view, the aim has to be to win the pool on your own.

I have won the Jackpot on many occasions, certainly more than a dozen times, and the Scoop6 five times, but I haven't always ended up ahead. The first time I won it was in August 2002. There was a rollover of £842,623 and, after deductions, over £1,322,000 was there to be won. Mark and I started off with a perm that came to £72,000 and trimmed it down to just under £10,000. The good news was that we had two winning tickets, the bad news that there were 255 other winning tickets, each paying £5,146. There was a bonus fund of over £686,000 to aim for the following Saturday, but we didn't win it, so our profit, after a lot of toil and tension, was a few hundred pounds.

My biggest Jackpot win was £268,643, at Haydock on 5 August 2004. There was over £567,000 in the pool that glorious day, and only 1.5 winning tickets, with Mark and me sharing one of them. When Look At The Stars won the third race, a median auction race for two-year-olds, at 16-1, almost everyone else was knocked out. Trained by Clive Cox, Look At The Stars had finished ninth in a maiden race at Windsor on its only previous appearance, and wasn't going to figure in many people's perms. Two races later, Mrs Moh went in at 12-1, to seal our triumph.

When you do a Tote Jackpot bet, it is worth bearing in mind that if there is a short-priced favourite, it will effectively be an even shorter price in the Jackpot pool, because just about everyone will include it in their selections, often as a banker. In contrast, a once-raced two-year-old who is 16-1 in the ring, like Look At The Stars, will be 100-1 in the Jackpot pool, because hardly any punters will include it. Those are the horses that wipe everyone else's bets out, so if you think there is a weakness in the horses at the head of the market, a horse like that is worth putting in.

When I won that huge Jackpot, I was in Denmark on holiday with my wife. I got a phone call at five p.m. 'Are you sitting down?' Since it was Mark ringing, I didn't think anyone had died. It was just a matter of how much we'd won.

Mark is the only betting partner I've ever had. When I do Jackpots and Scoop6 bets, it's not as part of a big syndicate, it's just the two of us. I generally make the selections, and Mark examines the maths. We try to find a way in which our permutation will be unique. For instance, in a six-race

Jackpot we might have a perm made up of two bankers, one race with two selections, one with three, and two races with twelve selections. That is 864 lines, which isn't a huge perm when the pool is big, but it means that if we get our bankers right and there is an upset in one of the races in which we've got a dozen selections, there is a good chance that we won't be knocked out but everyone else will be. We adopt a similar approach for the Scoop6, but with a £2 minimum unit stake you have to be a bit more ruthless with your perm. Personally, I wish they'd scrap the place element of the bet and put that money in the win pool, but the high minimum stake does mean that if there is a 10-1 winner an awful lot of people are knocked out.

I will sometimes do the Tote Placepot, but generally only when I can envisage at least two favourites finishing unplaced. If the card includes a four-runner race and I think one of the two outsiders could win, I might only include those two horses in that race. If the Placepot costs me £600, it is similar to having a £300 bet on each of those two horses, which is obviously risky but promises to be rewarding if it comes off. For me, there has to be something in a Placepot bet that will get rid of a large chunk of other people's tickets, or it is not worth doing. On the card with the four-runner race, if one of the two outsiders won, that could do the trick.

★

Jonathan Sparke, who founded City Index in 1983, is generally credited with having invented sports spread betting, but Sporting Index, set up by Compton Hellyer and Lindsay McNeile in 1992, led the way in marketing spread betting and introduced it to a wider audience. The following year, Stuart Wheeler's IG Index joined in when branching out from financial spreads into sports spread betting.

My experience in the City meant that I was familiar with the way spread betting works, and I was having spread bets long before I turned professional at the end of 1993. Spread betting is a fantastic vehicle for punters, certainly on horseracing. In fact, I think it's the best vehicle there is for punting on horses. As far as I am concerned, spread betting firms have got no chance against me. They can't beat me, and I can't see how they ever will. I would back myself at long odds-on to beat their odds compilers, and that is in no way a criticism of the compilers. I've got the utmost respect for them because they are attempting a hopeless task. Not only have they got to price up a mass of markets, they've also got to put up a two-way price, and offer punters the chance of opting for either side of the price, buy or sell. Even with a fairly conservative spread, they are putting up so many markets and prices that I can pick them off when they get it wrong. The only problem for me is getting on.

I rarely play the winning distances market, but if I did I would only ever be a seller. People react to a spot of rain by thinking the finishers will be strung out like washing, but I've seen plenty of four-mile chases run in mud where the race is decided in a photo-finish. I like the double numbers market because it's easy for me to use my tissue to construct my own double numbers index, and I like the favourites index, although there is a certain lack of control in that market because a horse you expect to start favourite may not, which can upset your calculations. On several occasions I've cheered a winner home only to discover that there was a last minute 'flip-flop' of favourites, and I should have been cheering on the horse that finished second, or was unplaced. It isn't a great feeling.

In practice, I play mainly on the race indexes: 50 points for the winner, 25 for the second and 10 for the third, in races with less than twelve runners, and 50-30-20-10 points in races with twelve runners and over. You are offered a two-sided price on every horse, and I use my tissue and some fairly complicated mathematics to calculate the chance of each horse scoring 50, 25 or 10 points, or 50-30-20-10 in bigger fields. I'm essentially a buyer of horses on race indexes, and a buyer of favourites, although that's a market I play much less often. I once bought a horse for £200 at 3 on an index, which won me £9,400, and more than once I've backed three horses that finished first, second and third, making up 85 points.

I also like match bets, where two horses are selected in a match, with a maximum make-up of twelve lengths in Flat races and fifteen lengths over jumps. My approach is to try to find a horse I am keen to oppose, in which case it doesn't matter too much what the other horse is. If I feel strongly enough about the outcome of the match, I also don't mind too much how many lengths the horse I expect to finish in front has to give up to the other one on the spread. When I like the match, I'll keep betting as long as they'll let me.

That is the problem: they won't let me.

My account with Sporting Index got closed fairly

quickly, and we now play a game of cat and mouse. I know Richard Glynn, Sporting Index's chief executive, fairly well, and we get on well. We've had lunch together several times, and discussed reopening my account, but it has never been reopened. I remember one occasion at the Cheltenham Festival when I asked Wally Pyrah, Sporting Index's PR director, to reopen it, and he said, 'You know you can't have an account with us.' So I rang Glynn, who had invited me to a box with some old City friends of mine he also knew. They had been told they could have bets for themselves, but not for me. On the phone, I asked Glynn again what were the chances of opening an account? He said, 'I think there are 62 different definitions of the word "no". Which one do you want?'

So I use other people's accounts and am constantly looking for new people to bet for me in their name. The trouble is, Sporting Index know that I recruit people, and make a point of finding out who they are. It's not that difficult, because they haven't got a big enough client base for my bets to get lost in it, and they know my style and pattern of betting, as well as that of the people whose accounts I use. I'm a creature of habit, essentially a buyer of horses on an index, horses that might be around 6-1 or 8-1 in the fixed-odds market. Most of their punters buy the favourite or second favourite on their index, so if someone who usually backs favourites suddenly wants a bigger bet on a longer-priced horse, they are suspicious, because punters rarely change their pattern of betting. When I'm dealing under another person's name, the traders at the other end of the phone often know that it's me using a satellite account and sometimes they'll deliberately leave the phone line open so that I can hear them shout, '£100 buy so-and-so, at 12, for Nevison.'

As I said, I think it's difficult for spread betting firms to succeed, and I admire the ones that have. The fact that Ladbrokes and William Hill both got rid of their spread betting operations pretty quickly - Ladbrokes after only eighteen months - is a pretty strong indicator of how difficult it is to make a decent profit from it. Spread betting companies are also regulated by the Financial Services Authority, which makes life harder for them, not least because it means that their product is surrounded by warnings about how much you can lose, while traditional bookmakers can market their product with a message about how much you can win. From a business point of view, it is not very helpful for potential customers to be made nervous about the risks. Moreover, spread betting is a bit too complicated for a lot of punters, and isn't suitable for betting shops. I think that spread betting companies rely heavily on a small number of high-rolling mugs and rich compulsive gamblers, whose losses enable the whole thing to work. They compensate for the clever winning punters, like me.

In 1998 Ladbrokes Sporting Spreads was sold to IG Index, who acquired William Hill Index in 2001, the same year that City Index sold its sports spread betting division to Sporting Index. On the other hand, two new firms entered the market, Spreadex in 2000 and Cantor Sports the following year.

Spreadex was set up by Peter Harris, a wealthy

businessman and successful racehorse trainer who subsequently handed his training yard over to Walter Swinburn, his son-in-law, a top jockey who had recently retired. I knew both Harris and Jonathan Hufford, Spreadex's managing director, who had been a City broker. He asked me to help out on their racing desk by supplying them with my prices. I did it for a year, while continuing with my normal work, and had no complaints, but I was never going to be on the other side of the fence for long. I'm just not a bookmaker.

I have sometimes been paid by racecourse bookmakers to supply them with my tissue, but it doesn't really work for either of us. My tissue works perfectly for me because I back the horses that are bigger prices with bookmakers than on my tissue, but I am not always right. If my tissue price for a horse is 8-1, and the bookmaker who has bought my tissue puts it up on his board at 8-1, when everyone else has it at 7-1, and the horse wins, the bookmaker is likely to ask me, 'What's happened there, then, Dave?' To me, it was simply a horse that I wouldn't want to back unless it was at least 10-1, but to him it was a horse he'd laid because my tissue price was 8-1, and as it turned out, he shouldn't have laid it.

Spreadex is still with us, but there were a few hiccups in the early days. Someone once told me that when you launch a new betting business, the first hundred applicants for accounts are applicants you don't want. Fifty of them are the best punters around, who you can't beat, and the other half are knockers who don't pay. Some of the first staff Spreadex recruited weren't sufficiently familiar with the mathematics of spread betting, and some enormous clangers were dropped, partly because people weren't quick enough to adjust the prices when there was a market move.

It was while I was helping Spreadex that I met Mark Smith, my business partner, whom Spreadex had poached from Ladbrokes, and who now works for IG Index. That was in 2000, the year after Betfair was founded.

Betfair changed everything. A lot of people were intimidated by it at first, because it used decimal odds and presented punters with prices to back and prices to lay, which was something they were not familiar with. To me, it was just like looking at a Reuters screen in the City. There was no mystique about it at all, and I took to it like a duck to water. My main initial reaction, shared by several others, was, why didn't I think of that? I'd spent an important part of my working life staring at foreign exchange screens, showing two-sided prices for currencies. This was a natural progression.

Bookmakers screamed that betting exchanges were illegal and that laying horses was their preserve, but bookmaking has always been a conduit between punters. At one time bookmakers were the middle men between people who wanted to back a particular horse and people who wanted to oppose it. Bookmakers then started to set the prices themselves, and customers bet against them. They balanced their books by matching one punter's bet on one horse against another punter's bet on a different horse. What bookmakers really objected to about exchanges was the fact that someone had introduced a better product, the perfect betting product for punters, with very low margins. Bookmakers screamed about the reduced margins, but in commerce that is the way the cookie crumbles when better, cheaper products come along. The case the bookmakers argued was really a protectionist, almost a racketeering argument.

The big bookmakers had been used to the benefits of an oligopoly, if not a cartel, for decades and they naturally didn't like it when their control of the marketplace was threatened. I did. I loved it, particularly in the early days. The volumes and liquidity were much lower then than they are today, but the markets, although thin, were populated by failed punters who thought they could turn things around by becoming layers. If a horse was 25-1 with the bookmakers, these heroes would step in to offer 70-1, thinking it was an easy way to get £20 out of a horse. I'd go to Southwell and, in the ring, the five longest-priced horses in a race would all be 20-1 or 25-1. Then I'd go into the press room and log on to Betfair on my laptop and the same horses would all be 80-1, because the new layers thought that none of those horses could win, were totally price insensitive, and thought it didn't matter what odds they put up, because they would still get their £20, or whatever it was. A bookmaker who adopted that approach would soon go broke, and quite a lot of those layers must have done too.

The discrepancies between the prices in the ring and the prices on Betfair weren't very marked at the front end of the market and, after taking Betfair's commission into account, I found myself having most of my shorter-priced bets in the ring. It was towards the other end of the market that the exchanges came into their own for me. When Betfair claimed that its prices were 25 per cent better than the bookmakers' prices, the reality was that they were only slightly better for the market leaders but were much better at the thin end of the market, for outsiders.

Outsiders tend to be shorter than they should be with bookmakers because they are worried that if they push all the 33-1 shots out to 75-1, they won't take much more money but will sometimes get caught out by one which is 'live'. They'd rather not take the risk.

Someone on Betfair certainly got caught out on 2 August 2005 when, to my surprise, Boot 'n Toot, whom I had priced up at 33-1, was returned at 100-1 for the Brighton Challenge Cup. Charles Cyzer's horse shouldn't have been as long as that, and she certainly shouldn't have been offered at 320-1 on Betfair, but she was. I kept on offering to have £5 on it, at around 300-1, and my offer kept being accepted. In the end I had £50 on Boot 'n Toot, she won by a short-head, and I won £16,000. First I was giggling, then I was whooping and hollering.

A few months later, in November, when the writer Mike Atherton visited me during research for his book on gambling (*Gambling: A Story of Triumph and Disaster*), I had a similar experience. At the time, despite that win from heaven on Boot 'n Toot, I was going through my worst ever spell. I was at rock bottom. Atherton came to my flat, we went out for lunch, then he watched while I played at Southwell, on a dreaded banded stakes card. In the second race I'd put Ice and Fire in at 33-1 on my tissue, yet it was available on Betfair at 180-1. I got £22 on, it won at an SP of 80-1, and I won almost £4,000. Atherton and I were doing high fives in my living room.

What on earth possesses people to risk losing that much money for the sake of winning £22, less commission? It still happens sometimes, but recently I've felt that you don't get as many silly-priced outsiders winning.

It would be wrong to say that I never lay horses on Betfair, but I haven't won money by laying horses and am definitely a backer rather than a layer. That is partly because I have a wonderful talent for laying winners. I remember appearing as a guest on Attheraces at Wolverhampton in May 2002 and confidently informing the audience (hopefully it was a small one) that I had laid Haunt The Zoo. She promptly won by seven lengths, at 7-1. Several years later, in February 2006, I laid Glen Thyne at 50-1 to £30. Glen Thyne was trained by Kim Bailey, whose horses were badly out of form. Unfortunately, the other horses in Bailey's yard hadn't told Glen Thyne, who won at 28-1. Fancy risking, and losing, £1,500 on that, for the sake of £30. I have never felt so stupid.

Betfair is as close to a perfect system of betting as you can get, matching backers with layers and taking a small cut in the form of commission, but there is one flaw. I think the margins are so small that there is a danger that Betfair will eventually run out of layers.

For traditional bookmakers, the margin is their defence mechanism. The smaller the margins, the weaker their defences. If prices on Betfair are 25 per cent better for backers when compared with bookmakers' prices, which is what Betfair has claimed, then the prices must be roughly 25 per cent worse for layers. That makes the long-term future for layers on Betfair pretty bleak - unless you are a crook and know that the horse you are laying cannot win.

I don't believe that betting exchanges have made racing crooked when it wasn't crooked before, but they have facilitated the laying of horses, and that has created more opportunities for crooks. There have always been bookmakers prepared to lay a horse on someone else's behalf, perhaps someone who has spent a certain amount of time at Her Majesty's pleasure, and knows that the horse won't win. There have always been crooks in racing, and they are largely the same crooks as before, but Betfair has made it easier for them to lay horses.

Betfair say that betting can now be policed in a way it never has been before, because everything is recorded and the information is made available to the authorities, but they have made what was only available to relatively few people available to everyone - the facility to lay horses. The number of suspect races definitely increased when the exchanges arrived, and a few years ago, during winter meetings on the all-weather, it became laughable. The sort of day I have in mind is a day like that at Southwell on 17 February 2004. There were eight races, and in seven of them explanations were submitted for runs that were either unexpectedly good or bad. A dozen horses were the subject of official explanations. Horses were reported to have hung right, or hung left, or the jockey had steering problems on the bend, or a filly was subsequently found to be in season.

In the first race, The Fisio drifted alarmingly in the betting, although he still went off the 7-2 co-favourite, was slowly away and never got into the race. The official explanation was that the horse tried to duck under the starting gates. Later in the afternoon, Prince Of Blues drifted badly in the market before finishing last, at 9-1. The explanation was that the horse hit its head on the stalls. I am not saying that the explanations were not true or valid, but days like that made me increasingly suspicious because the market seemed to be able to predict an imminent mishap. I wrote at the time, 'Looking a gift horse in the mouth is certainly the best of options these days.'

The following winter, I suggested that if a horse running on an all-weather track drifted by more than two points on Betfair, especially if it was the forecast favourite in that morning's *Racing Post*, there was a good chance that it would either miss the break, race wide, or provide an opportunity to watch a jockey making flapping motions with his elbows.

It wasn't just the betting exchanges that caused me to be suspicious, it was also the introduction of banded racing for bad horses. A lot of jockeys have their punters, the prize money isn't worth running for, and it was an open invitation to crookery. If racing is about making money, and you can't make money by playing the game straight, the obvious option is to play the game bent, and some people were definitely doing that.

The situation has now improved, mainly because the authorities have tightened things up and taken much-publicised action against some of the culprits. I've always thought that the jockeys most susceptible to being involved in hookey races are apprentices whose careers have gone downhill, perhaps because of weight problems, and twilight jockeys nearing the end of their careers. A young apprentice who has known success but is now struggling to make a living can be vulnerable, and so can a jockey who knows things aren't going to get better, and wants to boost his retirement fund. I think that Gary Carter, who was 40 when he was disqualified for five years, in 2005, for having supplied information for reward, was an example of a jockey in a vulnerable position. The Jockey Club's disciplinary panel did not charge Carter with stopping horses but, in respect of eight rides, concluded that 'at its lowest, he did not ride them to achieve the best possible result'.

There are some jockeys I used to watch and, when I looked at their mounts, think to myself, will this one be trying, or is it one for another day? Some older jockeys are masters at stopping a horse without having obviously appeared to do so, and later that year I saw what I regarded as a particularly bad case of non-trying. The horse opened at a much longer price than I had him in my tissue, but it seemed that the more I put on, the more his price drifted. I ended up having over £1,000 on the horse, which was a lot for the kind of race he was running in, and I was suspicious. He was slowly away and wasn't asked for an effort until it was too late. The jockey was suspended by the local stewards but cleared on appeal. All I can say is that I'll go to my grave convinced that the local stewards got it right.

I'd love to know if there is a correlation between horses that drift in the betting and those that start slowly, because the start offers a perfect opportunity to get things off to a . . . well, a bad start. My natural cynicism suggests to me that there probably is a correlation.

CHAPTER EIGHT

HOW DO I DO IT?

The partnership with Mark Smith began while we were both working for Spreadex, although at that time it was just a case of exchanging ideas, each of us telling the other when he fancied something, and backing it for ourselves if we wanted to. Then we started having cuts of each other's bets, and gradually it became a more formal arrangement. Mark is a sports trader with IG Index, whereas I am not at all interested in sports other than horseracing, so there was a division of labour along those lines, with Mark generally deferring to my opinion on horses, and me following him on sports.

Mark had learnt how markets and bookmakers work and is good at predicting movements in the market. Nowadays it's a very competitive marketplace, and if you can get on at the best prices, you've got a good chance of winning. Mark helps me do that. He will look at special offers on place terms – perhaps a bookmaker is offering one quarter the odds the first five to attract customers – or at markets where they are betting without the favourite, novelty markets, anything where we might be able to get an edge.

At a big meeting like the Cheltenham Festival, the market is so competitive that if we can put a line through horses that represent 15 per cent of the book in a race and combine the others in various ways, we are certain to make a profit. Some days during the Festival I look at the card and know that I am going to win. Then I just want to get as much on as I can. I will get my tissue out and work out where the value lies, and Mark will trawl and scour the screens, endlessly, looking for different ways of exploiting my judgements. It's a case of trying to press home our advantage, or what we believe is our advantage.

If everything went as wrong as it possibly could at the Cheltenham Festival, we'd probably be finished, because our turnover there is huge. Our worst day was when we lost £15,000, although that included a losing Jackpot bet. Everything seemed to conspire against us, but, mercifully, it is rare for us to lose five-figure sums. Normally, if we have laid out that sort of money, it means we have a lot of bases covered. When the coin is spinning in the air, it almost has to land on its edge for us to be completely defeated. For instance, we might have a match bet where we want horse A to finish in front of horse B, but also have another match bet in which we want horse B to beat horse C. We hope to end up with two winning bets and are fairly unlikely to end up with two losing ones. An industry professional could pick apart what we do and find holes in it, and we've certainly had bets that are embarrassing to own up to – what punter hasn't? – but the whole package works for us, which is what matters in the end.

We have a lot of bets that other professional punters would regard as irrational, and which we don't expect to win, because they are 80-1 or 100-1 shots. At least, we don't expect them to win very often. They don't need to. They only need to win more than one time in 80, or 100, to have been worthwhile.

When I was working for The Winning Line, I was always being asked what my strike rate was. Well, I couldn't give a fig about my strike rate. If all your bets are on horses at prices between 11-10 and 7-4, your strike rate matters; but if, like me, you back an even-money chance one day and a 100-1 chance the next, your strike rate is pretty much irrelevant.

Most punters bet within a price range that suits them, and 100-1, or even 33-1, is outside most punters' price range, because they can't bear all those 33-1 losers. I back a lot of 33-1 losers, and quite a lot of 100-1 losers, probably more on sports bets, following Mark, than on horses, and it works for us.

Since I've got no real interest in sports other than horseracing, Mark doesn't usually bother to tell me what we've backed until the event's over – unless, say, we've backed two golfers at long prices, and on Sunday evening, in the final round of a PGA tournament, they are in contention. One Sunday in January 2002 Mark rang and said, 'Are you watching the darts?' I wasn't. 'Well, we're on this haemophiliac Australian player at 100-1 for the Embassy World Darts Championship, and he's doing well.' My two sons sat on my knee and we watched the telly and shouted Tony David on.

'One hundred and eighty!'

Amazingly, he won, despite his haemophilia – not an ideal condition for a darts player.

Sometimes, if I'm not doing anything with the kids on a Sunday afternoon and a soccer game comes on at four p.m., I'll ring Mark and ask if we've got an interest in the match. If we haven't, I'll say, 'Put a hundred on something,' just for something to watch. It's not an approach recommended by most professionals, but unless I've got a betting interest I've got no interest at all in sports events. It's the same with horseracing. I freely confess that, for me, the appeal of horseracing is the betting, not the horses or the racing. If I'm not betting, or talking about betting, you won't find me at a racecourse.

★

A lot of people like the idea of being a professional punter, but I don't think most of them realise how much work goes into it, or how much emotional energy (though I hope you have a good idea by now). It's a full-time job, and not an easy one. It is certainly not simply a matter of looking at the card in the morning, studying the form, making a few selections, backing them, watching them run, then working out how much richer you are. It is hard work, and it has become harder and harder over the years, particularly because we have to use a number of different accounts to get our bets on. It's a constant frustration that I can't just bowl up to a bookmaker, present myself as Dave Nevison, and back a horse at the best price, but it's a fact of life that I can't. As a result, Mark and I have an inordinate amount of money sitting in a lot of accounts. The money's somewhere, but it's certainly not in our pockets, and when someone has put a bet on for me, I can wait months to get paid.

Nowadays, after a week's racing I'm often knackered and am well aware that I find it harder to keep on top of the form than I used to. There's so much of it, which is why, recently, I've started to focus more on jump racing, as I did in the early days, but for a different reason. There is less form to study than on the Flat, so I can keep on top of it more easily.

I used to want to pore over 0-60 handicaps at Brighton

and got a real kick out of it when I got it right. However, the reality was that I'd often spend two hours studying some awful race at Southwell and still get it wrong. Now, I won't waste my time trying to solve what is often an impossible puzzle. Anyway, it is demoralising looking at a bunch of horses that rarely or never win, and deciding what value to place on the fact that one of them finished tenth last time out, while another one finished ninth, in an equally dreadful race somewhere else.

I realise that, at 45, I can't work or play as hard as I once could, and it would kill me to work every day of the week. Now, I take time off, which used to be anathema to me, unthinkable. It's become essential. I'll concentrate on the big days, then take a break when the racing is poor, which it often is. I always did take an annual holiday with my family, usually after Glorious Goodwood, to glorious Cornwall, and made a point of leaving my mobile phone behind, but the pain of missing a winner while I was away was awful, worse than backing a loser. I'd get back home, look at the results in the *Racing Post*, then cry. Missing a winner used to drive me mad, even though I had probably missed backing a betting slip full of losers as well. You don't notice those.

Mark has also cut down on the number of events he bets on, and tends to focus on the big events where there are a lot of different betting angles to exploit, such as the golf majors.

I think Mark and I are good at what we do, but we've certainly benefited from the fact that the betting industry has become so much more competitive than it used to be. If the market was still totally dominated by Ladbrokes, William Hill and Coral; if there was still off-course betting duty and deductions of 9 per cent (they seem a world away now); and if the internet hadn't arrived, we might not have succeeded. Equally, in the future it could change in ways that make life more difficult for us. The government might introduce a tax on gambling winnings, or change the regulatory system in an unhelpful way, or bookmakers might change their place terms. That could have a big impact on us, and it could very well happen.

There's one punter I know who regularly rings me up to complain that he can't get his bet on with a major bookmaker, but, although I could easily knock the big bookmakers, I don't really have that many complaints. It's true that if I ask for a £25 each-way yankee on the day's big races, quite a few bookmakers will cut me down to £10 each-way, which makes me think they're not proper bookmakers. If a big bookmaker displays a price, it should mean that the company wants to lay it, not refuse to lay it. The one extenuating circumstance is if the horse is Pricewise's selection in the *Racing Post* and the firm is offering the longest price about the horse, because Pricewise has a big following and there will be a tremendous amount of money for his selection. Some bookmakers react better than others in that situation. To be fair to them, I think William Hill are very good and Ladbrokes and Corals are pretty good; better, I think, than Victor Chandler. I have developed good relationships with the bookmakers' racecourse representatives and nowadays will quite often bet through them. The only one who won't take a bet from me is Damian Walker, the Tote's representative.

At a big festival meeting I will often have a multiple bet, perhaps a £100 each-way yankee or a £200 each-way trixie, and have it at SP, for two reasons. First, it makes it much easier to get the bet on, and second, SP margins are less than the margins in the early price markets. It means I don't have to split the bet up into smaller pieces and spread it around, but can actually put it on under my own name. Unless the bet includes a horse whose price I think will go through the floor, in which case I'll want to take an early price about it, I think I'm usually better off taking the SP. If the first two horses in a multiple bet go in at long prices then the bookmakers will take action to shorten up the SP of the remaining horses; but in that situation I'll be looking to lay them on Betfair anyway.

I will spend extra time studying handicaps with sixteen or more runners because bookmakers pay one quarter the odds the first four places when the mathematics suggests that they shouldn't. If I like two horses at 6-1 and 8-1 in a sixteen-runner handicap, I will back them both each-way, often quite heavily, but you can't do that easily on the racecourse, where the each-way market is dead and bookmakers become less friendly if you start backing too many 6-1 shots with them, each-way.

I rarely fall out with anyone in the ring, but Martyn of Leicester, who bets each-way, will shout out, 'David, good to see you. Does the phone not work any more? Welcome to

the betting ring. Can I interest you in anything each-way?'
To be fair to him, he does lay a bet to good money, and
Colin Webster, on the rails, takes each-way bets. I think he
does it as a loss-leader, to attract the bigger players. He
probably loses on the place bets but gets those punters' win
bets, as well, and makes a profit on those.

Betfair has exposed the fact that bookmakers' place terms
are wrong. If you look at the place odds on Betfair they
represent the chances of a horse being placed far more
accurately than the bookmakers' place terms. The big high-
street bookmakers will deny it, but I think they effectively
operate a loose cartel and will eventually all change their
place terms together, perhaps by offering one fifth the odds
where now they offer one quarter, and maybe one sixth the
odds where it is now one fifth.

If bookmakers' prices differ, market forces quickly bring
them into line, but I still think there must be an element of
collusion between them over their early prices. I know that
if you ask two respected judges to price up the same eight-
runner race, they will often produce remarkably different
tissues. My starting point for reading the form is John
Whitley's figures, while Eddie Fremantle's is Raceform and
his own speed figures, but that doesn't wholly explain why
we often arrive at totally different conclusions, with
enormous variance in our prices. Yet if you look at the
bookmakers' prices in Pricewise, in the *Racing Post*,
the variation in each horse's odds is very limited. It is
the similarity of their starting point prices that makes
me think there must be some collusion between the

major bookmakers. If there wasn't, they would keep getting picked off when they were seriously out of line with the rest of the market.

Mark and I will carry on doing what we are doing, while being alert to changes and the possible need to adapt. People who watch us at the racecourse and in the press room don't get a true picture of our operation, because they only see part of it. Someone may see us lose £5,000 in cash, but the bet that really mattered may have been a multiple bet or Jackpot bet placed off-course. If someone who I don't know, or don't like, comes up and asks how I'm doing, I always tell them that I've done my money. If you tell people how much you've won, the conversation drags on, and you make enemies, because some people don't really like the fact that you make money betting, when they probably don't. If someone I know, and who knows how I operate, asks how things are going, I'll tell them things could be better, but could be worse, and that we're in front. I'm not ashamed to admit that, month after month, year after year, we're in front, but I choose who to admit it to. It definitely irks some people, including people who have an awful lot of knowledge about racing but bet themselves into trouble, which is probably why they are irritated by my success.

The real give-away as to whether a professional punter is in front or behind is whether or not he is still to be seen at a racecourse – unless he's abandoned the betting ring for Betfair. If you stop turning up, it usually means that you're behind; and if you disappear for a while, it means you are behind and owe money. If you are still turning up, you are probably doing OK.

★

Punters are much better informed than they used to be, but it is questionable whether or not they are better at using the information. Knowledge isn't enough. It is at least as important to know what to do with the knowledge. There are people who know the form better than I do, but they couldn't produce a useful tissue, nor spot a bet if it hit them over the head.

The tissue is the engine room of our operation. Everything depends on the merit of my tissue. If it's not good enough, I'm going to be out of business. I have to put a price next to every horse in a race because all of them contribute something towards the final percentage figure of 100. It's a difficult process to explain because it has become second nature to me. Normally, I start by identifying the likely favourite. If I think there are good reasons for thinking it might be beaten, then I'll put it in my tissue at a price that is probably longer than in the newspapers, or in the bookmakers' early prices, which means that there should be some value available about other horses in the race. If I can't see a way of beating the favourite, and I put it in at a price shorter than in the newspaper, it may mean that I end up backing it. If I am wrong about the favourite, it means I am wrong about other horses, too, and when I compare my tissue with the forecast prices in the paper, or with Betfair's prices, I sometimes feel either very good about it, or I suspect I've made a terrible mistake. I'm either gloriously right or horribly wrong, and I will look at the race again to see whether or not I still feel the same way.

It is hard to divorce yourself completely from the *Racing Post*'s betting forecast. It is very easy to become lazy and, if I have put a horse in at 8-1 when the *Racing Post* has it at 14-1, simply push my price out to 10-1, which isn't a logical thing to do. Putting a percentage figure by each horse's name, and feeling confident about it, isn't easy either. I start with John Whitley's sheets of figures in front of me. They help highlight the circumstances associated with a horse showing its peak form: the course and distance, the going, the jockey, and so on. Then I check to see if the same set of circumstances are in place today.

I'm not a great one for collateral form, for noting that A was giving B 5lb when beating him three lengths a month ago, while C was giving B 8lb when beating him one length two weeks later, then paying a lot of attention to how many pounds better or worse off each one is compared with the other. I think that approach is outdated. I'm likely to attach more weight to the fact that a number of conditions today are similar to when a horse performed in a particular way before, so there is a good chance it will reproduce that performance. Having said that, I certainly don't ignore the weight a horse is carrying, and I believe that horses reach a ceiling. If a horse is running off its highest-ever handicap mark, I want to see what it has done to justify that mark, and try to decide whether its latest rating is a stepping stone to an even higher one, or represents the limit of its ability.

My confidence in my tissue is greater for some types of

race than for others. For instance, I prefer races with older horses, where the horses' form is exposed and their running tends to follow a reasonably predictable pattern. Certain horses can win off a handicap mark of 69 but not off 72; other horses only win when ridden by a jockey, not by a 7lb claiming apprentice; others need a particular kind of pace in a race to show their best form, and pace is one of the things I pay a lot of attention to. I'm not the only person who finds races with a lot of established performers easier to assess, so the margins in those races are small, but there are still enough times when my prices are out of kilter with the bookmakers to make me particularly fond of them.

If it's a twenty-runner handicap, I'll want to put a line through eight of the runners. Either the distance is wrong, or the going is unsuitable, or I don't like the rider, or the draw is unhelpful. One way or another, a line has to be put through eight of them. You've got to be fairly ruthless, and keep narrowing it down. My approach to any race is to weed out the horses I think can't win.

Quite often, an all-aged handicap on the Flat will include some improving three-year-olds. I think the best position to adopt when faced by an improving three-year-old is to take the view that it won't improve as much as people think it will. There's a tendency to think that, if a horse is improving, hacked up in its last race, is trained by Sir Michael Stoute, and only has to improve another 10lb to win again, then it's worth backing. Some trainers are masters at training horses to improve through the ranks, and a few times every year I get caught out by an improving three-year-old trained by

Stoute, or Sir Mark Prescott, or Luca Cumani, but very few horses are capable of improving by 20lb in a season. Most horses let you down, and I am happy to err on the side of believing that a horse won't improve massively.

Instead, I tend to look for a horse who, given that the circumstances of the race suit it, is likely to repeat a previous performance. I am looking for horses to do what they have done before, under similar conditions. Sometimes, of course, the horse I back will be beaten by an improving three-year-old who has improved again. They do win and they need to win sometimes to keep punters backing them, but their reputation affects their price and they are invariably a shorter price than they should be. For me, the horse with a reputation is the one that is there to be beaten.

As I said, many knowledgeable punters, even if their form judgement is sound, simply don't know how to translate their knowledge into profit. They don't know what bet to have, which is where working with Mark helps me. We both have pretty sharp mathematical minds, but two minds are better than one when it comes to identifying the best ways of exploiting knowledge. If, for instance, I don't fancy two of the forecast favourites, and have them both at 8-1 in my tissue, we have to decide whether it's best to simply lay both of them, or back several other horses against them, or look for other ways in which we can most lucratively oppose those two favourites.

Gambling is not just a mental test, of course, it is also an emotional test. Emotion plays a massive part in my betting. I don't have any rules, and when I have a strong gut feeling that

I'm right about something, I'm not afraid to step way above my normal mark and really try to knock it out of the ground. It was like that with Kelami in the William Hill Trophy Handicap Chase at Cheltenham in 2005. It was the first day of the Festival meeting. I'd worked on the card the night before, and in the morning, when I saw that François Doumen's horse, ridden by Robert Thornton, was 10-1, I thought he was a good bet. Sitting in the back seat of the car on the way to the racecourse, I kept looking at the race, and thinking about it, and the more I looked at it and thought about it, the more strongly I felt that Kelami was an absolute good thing. I had £2,500 each-way at 10-1. When Kelami won, I won over £30,000, and I've won similar amounts on several other occasions when I've had the same gut feeling about a horse.

Naturally, there have been times when the outcome hasn't been as enjoyable, but I think one of my strengths is that I am pretty good at putting a bad result behind me and getting back to work. There are plenty of punters who will be in a pub on a Thursday night still talking about the one that was beaten in a photo-finish at Windsor the previous Monday, since when they'll have gone on the chase and backed another dozen losers. I have the ability to draw a line under each day's events. I might cry about something that has gone against me – perhaps when a horse I have backed to win (when I should have backed it each-way) gets beaten on the line, or when a jockey messes it up, and I've lost several thousand pounds – but I am able to move on, telling myself that there will be days when I have the chance to get the money back. Some people's whole lives seem to be clouded by one awful betting experience that they can't get out of their minds, but I don't think many people would be able to tell whether I've had a bad day or a good day. I don't let it gnaw away at me. That isn't to say that in my quieter moments I don't agonise about setbacks and bad runs, but I know that it is in my own interests to stay positive, otherwise you are beaten before you start.

I can't understand people who go racing and tell you that they've got £50 to lose, and clearly expect to lose it. If that's the way they think, why not save time and throw the money out of the car window now? Better still, give it to me, because I'm going to win. Betting is partly a state of mind. If you are positive about it, feel on top of it, and have money, you are more likely to win than if you have just had a phone call from your wife to tell you that there's a bill for £10,000 for school fees that needs to be paid when you get home. That's a good way of guaranteeing that you're about to go three grand down. I think the saying 'scared money never wins' is true.

Despite my ability to deal with betting misfortunes, things do happen that trigger bad betting behaviour. Even after all these years I'm still not immune to chasing losses – an almost universal affliction among punters.

I hate betting at bank holiday meetings, so on an August bank holiday Monday in 2006 I was perfectly happy to be at Epsom with Racing UK. I'd done a tissue for the card, put a line through it because it was a 'no bet' card, and was looking forward to getting paid £200 for a relaxing afternoon without any betting action.

The first race was a seven-runner median auction maiden stakes for two-year-olds. I went to look at them in the parade ring behind the stands. The second favourite was tiny and looked as if she hadn't eaten for a month, while the favourite, Loch Tay, who had run well on his debut at Newmarket and was ridden by Frankie Dettori for Michael Bell, looked like Motivator, Bell's Derby winner. Bell's son, fresh out of private school and wet behind the ears, told me Loch Tay should win. It was then that I got on the phone and put £300 on it at evens. Loch Tay came down the hill like a rattlesnake, going from one side of the track to the other, and never looked like winning.

Three hundred on an even-money shot is a small bet for me, but it knocked me off balance because it was such a stupid thing to have done. Having come with the intention of not having a bet, I'd promptly lost more than I was being paid for working all afternoon. Worse still, after thirteen years as a professional punter, I'd allowed myself to be influenced by a schoolboy. What sort of pillock was I?

Apparently the sort who, having stupidly lost £300, then loses another two grand trying to get it back. Bad days aren't always the result of having got my tissue wrong; they are sometimes the result of doing something stupid, then making it worse. Having lost £300, I knew that I was going to have more bets. I don't know whether or not it was compulsive behaviour, but it was certainly wrong, and I paid for it.

Two races later, I was discussing a twelve-runner sprint handicap on Racing UK and got it absolutely spot on. I suggested it was between three horses, Bond City, Cape

Royal, and Jayanjay. They finished in that order, separated by half a length and a neck – and I backed the second and third. Sometimes it happens like that, but the important thing is to get over it quickly. That day I did get over it, but not until I'd lost over £2,000. Idiot.

On the other hand, I think I'm generally at my best when the north face of the Eiger is in front of me, and I need to climb it to pay all the bills. When I'm in a comfort zone, and everything is going swimmingly, I invariably have a wobbly spell when I don't seem to have my eye on the ball or my foot on the pedal properly. If I ever had a couple of million to spare I'd have to stop gambling altogether, because if I didn't, I know I'd lose the lot. This isn't a game you can win by playing part-time or half-heartedly. You have to be immersed in it, and one of the things I am proud of is that, somehow, I do manage to maintain a social life as well as going to the races every day and backing horses for a living.

The proof of the pudding, as the cliché goes, is in the eating, in which case Mark and I have baked a pretty good pudding. I'm not sure of the exact dimensions of the pudding I baked before joining forces with Mark because I've never kept accounts, which will horrify most professional punters. I'm sure that virtually all other professional gamblers keep a meticulous record of their bets, and a profit and loss account, but I never have. I know the orthodox view is that it's essential to keep your betting money separate from your other finances, or you'll be in big trouble, but my betting funds just slosh around with the rest of my money in various accounts. My approach is simple: if there's anything in the bank at the end of the month after everything has been paid, I'm doing all right; if there isn't, I'm not. I reckon I was making about £50,000 a year in the late 1990s, and rather more than that over the next few years. However much I made, it was enough to build a large, architect-designed house in Kent, and for my family and me to live very comfortably.

The partnership with Mark got going properly in 2002 which, up until then, was my most profitable year. Mark is my straight man and accountant, and all the bets we have together, which account for about two thirds of all my bets, are recorded in his books. Working with Mark definitely gave a big boost to my profits. In 2003 we made about £260,000, and the following year, £325,000. In 2005 – ah, in 2005 we won £4,000, which was disastrous. Remember, I'm a professional punter. Although I also write and broadcast, punting is what I rely on for my living, and my living, with a wife from whom I am separated, and four children, doesn't come cheap. A hundred grand a year wouldn't cover it, so £4,000 was a big step towards the end of life as a professional punter and the start of life as something else – a pauper, perhaps. It isn't all cakes and ale. This is what happened.

★

Actually, I don't really fully understand what did happen, except that it all went horribly, almost terminally wrong.

People kept telling me that I was one of the last professional punters left on the racecourse. All the others were supposedly sitting at home making millions on Betfair. Lotte and I had recently split up and I was looking for ways of making it easier to see my children, so in September 2005 I decided, for business and personal reasons, to bet from home. It seemed to make good sense. Instead of dashing off to catch a train every morning and spending many hours, and a lot of money, travelling to distant racecourses, I could spend more time in the peace and quiet of home, studying the races and pricing them up.

Unfortunately it didn't work like that, and I might have guessed it wouldn't because I'd tried it on a smaller scale before. During the winter of 2002-03 I decided to stop travelling to meetings at Wolverhampton, which sometimes involved setting off at seven a.m. and not getting home until 11 p.m., and bet from home. The winter before that I'd won £30,000 at Wolverhampton; betting from home, I managed to lose £30,000.

During those final months of 2005 I'd gladly have settled for a £30,000 loss. At home, my work ethic seemed to suffer alarmingly. Having to catch a train at a particular time gave structure to my mornings. Now I got up, turned the television on, lazed around and kept telling myself that there were still three hours until the first race. I told myself I'd get started in half an hour's time. Then Jerry Springer would appear on the television screen, and I'd watch an awful-looking creature talk about the day when she discovered her husband was a transvestite and his best friend was actually his gay lover, followed by a great fat man arguing with his girlfriend about how many burgers he ate. Before long I had become a couch potato, and when I finally stirred myself the first race would be twenty minutes away.

I'd sit down in a frenzy with the *Racing Post*, my head going round in circles, and not be properly prepared. I'd stare at the prices on the computer screen. If I'd backed a horse on Betfair at 8.2 and it drifted to 10.1, I'd think there was a conspiracy to defeat me. It was all demons and devils. Maybe I was spending too much time on my own, away from the familiar surroundings of the racecourse. Maybe I went slightly mad, or maybe it was just a bad run.

Every punter, amateur and professional, has good and bad runs, and Mark and I had avoided a bad run for a long time. We were certainly due one, and in 2005 we got one. I'm reluctant to accept that ours was due to the change in my personal circumstances, but it was a difficult time for me, a time when my life was changing, and it coincided with a change in my approach to betting. Perhaps the fact that our results went downhill wasn't a coincidence. I don't know.

Anyway, I found myself agonising over the decisions I'd made, over my prices, selections and bets. But even then I didn't find myself blaming my decisions. I didn't feel that I had suddenly lost it, and that my judgement had failed. I'd look back on another bad day and usually conclude that there was nothing much wrong with my prices or decisions. It was just a bad run. The trouble was, a few more thousand pounds had leaked out of our betting accounts.

The bad run actually started before I abandoned the racecourse. Rising Cross, the racehorse I part-owned, was doing us proud, but the horses I was backing weren't. On the Friday of supposedly Glorious Goodwood, 29 July 2005, I managed to back the first five runners-up and had my biggest each-way bet of the week on Roodeye, at 20-1, in the ten-runner Oak Tree Stakes. She was beaten a short-head into fourth place. Two hours later I backed Prince Namid at Thirsk, at 100-1. He was beaten half a length. It was an experience I was about to become very familiar with.

Over the next few months there were an awful lot of near misses and a lot of the ones that really mattered were in Jackpots and Scoop6s. If some of them had hit the back of the net instead of the front of the crossbar, the year might have ended up very differently. I have always looked down my nose at punters who complain that they are unlucky, but by the end of 2005 I was beginning to change my mind on that front. I cursed my own luck.

In the second week of August I made a very welcome five-figure profit, much of it thanks to having kept the faith with Linden's Lady in a selling race at Thirsk, despite the fact that she drifted badly in the market. On the Saturday there was £700,000 in the Scoop6 win fund and would soon be almost £200,000 in the Jackpot. We risked what we had won during the week to go for both, and went out of both in the first leg, with Appalachian Trail sinking the Newbury Jackpot by a head.

After losing at York's Ebor meeting, I set off for a few days' holiday with my family, to Torquay. On the Tuesday, 23 August, there was another worthwhile Jackpot carryover at Yarmouth, and I couldn't resist having a go. In the morning, I dispatched the kids to the hotel swimming pool, to annoy the elderly, and repaired to the bar to study the form. During the afternoon, Lotte and I went for a walk around the harbour. Every 30 minutes I disappeared to listen to the next race. It wasn't very convincing, and eventually Lotte suggested that either I was suffering from a particularly severe attack of diarrhoea or my assurance that it would be a non-betting holiday wasn't worth the betting slip it was written on. There was nothing else for it but to confess, making clear that the good news was that, after four legs, our bet was still alive. Lotte didn't seem to regard this as cause for celebration and, as it turned out, it wasn't. We won the Jackpot, but so did 70 other ticket holders, each winning ticket paying £1,210. We got back £400 less than we had put in.

Two days later I drove us home with unseemly haste and arrived back just in time to back Thoughtsofstardom in a nursery at Musselburgh. After 100 yards he jinked and unseated Joe Fanning. At least that Sunday, when I took the family to Goodwood, we had the thrill of watching Rising Cross finish runner-up to Nannina in the Group 3 Prestige Stakes.

A month later, on Sunday, 25 September, at Newmarket, there was another big Jackpot pool, almost £428,000. We negotiated the first five races successfully, including Leo at 8-1 and Baron's Pit at 20-1. In the final leg we had King's Majesty, the favourite, as a banker. He was beaten a head. And then things really began to go wrong. At Goodwood on 9 October we had the winners of the first four legs, and of the last, and had five of the nine runners in the Harvest Handicap, including Signatory. He was beaten a neck by Alessano. The Jackpot wasn't won that day, and by the time it reached Wetherby on Wednesday, 12 October, it was heading towards a £520,000 pool. After five races, including winners at 10-1 and 11-2, our flag was still flying, and since we had five of the thirteen runners in the final leg on our side, including five of the six market leaders, we were pretty hopeful. Stoneravinmad did for us, by a length, at 16-1.

A month later, Leicester, Monday, 14 November, another Jackpot, another five out of six. Ten days later, Taunton, the first five legs safely negotiated, and five of the ten runners for the closing handicap hurdle in our perm. Unfortunately, they didn't include Devito, the 14-1 winner. Nor did anyone else's perm, with the result that when racing started at Newbury the next day, there was already over £175,000 in the pool. Again, we had the first five winners. In the last, we had the odds-on favourite, Heltornic, and the second favourite, Bonchester Bridge. Ballyhoo won, at 28-1.

It was getting beyond a joke. The crossbar was in splinters. On some of these trying days Mark and I got our stake back and sometimes a bit more by laying our last race selections on Betfair, but if we'd won one of those Jackpots it would have put me back in the game.

But that is the nature of Jackpots. Recently someone told me that he was thinking of giving them up because he had got five out of six several times. I told him that if he was getting five out of six he should keep going, because there was a good chance that he would eventually get six out of six. It's if you keep getting three out of six that you should stop, although I don't need to be told how frustrating near misses are. Time after time, Mark and I went desperately close but just couldn't quite get it right. It was a real test of our partnership, and, perhaps because we had enjoyed so much success for so long, we didn't fall out or even have disagreements, which was pretty remarkable.

During the last four months of 2005 I lost about £250,000, which wiped out all the profit from the previous eight months, and nearly wiped me out completely. What Mike Atherton didn't realise when we were doing high fives after Ice and Fire had won at Southwell, and I'd won almost £4,000, was that if it had lost, my Betfair account would have been empty. I was down to the last knockings. Atherton probably thought he was watching a genius at work, but I was thinking about ways of raising money because I hadn't any liquid assets left. I wasn't in serious financial trouble because it never reached the stage where I owed money, and I had a lot of equity in property, but it was getting near the end of the line in terms of carrying on as a professional punter. Maybe Lotte's original prediction was finally about to come true.

During the run-up to Christmas 2005, Mark and I had a crisis meeting. It consisted largely of me telling Mark that I hadn't got any money left. The answer was to go back to doing what suited me best: working on the racecourse. Somehow, I am better when there is some human interaction, when I can actually see the whites of the bookmakers' eyes. Sitting in front of a computer screen on my own all day just doesn't work for me.

★

I had managed to make a good living in the betting ring when SP margins averaged well over 2 per cent per runner.

Now, thanks partly to Betfair and to the Levy Board's decision in 2003 to allow racecourse bookmakers to hedge with betting exchanges, margins were down to about 1.5 per cent per runner. It was a huge difference. I knew I could win, and I needed to, badly.

Margins first started falling when the betting ring was reformed, in 1998, and pitch positions could be bought and sold. The ring needed modernising, but with the other changes that have taken place, all making the betting market much more competitive, it wouldn't surprise me if racecourse bookmakers disappear during my lifetime. When pitches first became available, a lot of young would-be bookmakers stepped in, and most of them soon stepped out again, because betting on the racecourse is not a route to riches, as they imagined, but a way of life.

Some of the newcomers simply didn't know what they were doing. At Ascot, one of the new bookmakers decided that the way to attract money was simply to offer better prices than the bookmakers on either side of him. He succeeded in attracting money, but the outcome wasn't quite what he had expected. Eventually a neighbouring layer, not very amused, went up to him and asked, 'Are you sure you know what you're doing? You are betting to 95 per cent on your board.' 'I know,' replied the newcomer, 'but they've still got to pick the winner.' Another new arrival, who thought he'd got a pitch at Ayr for a bargain price, discovered a particular local difficulty. The bookmaker next to him, who has since died, was regularly betting overbroke, which made life unbearable for his new neighbour. Eventually, the new bookmaker invited his nemesis for a drink and asked him why he was betting overbroke. 'Hasn't anyone told you?' he replied. 'I don't want to win.' His main job was not bookmaking, but money laundering.

In Scotland, where there is no shortage of punters, there is more variation in the prices on bookmakers' boards than in England, perhaps because a lot of people with other businesses have racecourse pitches as a sideline, and bet to their opinions rather than try to balance their book. In Ireland, the racecourse bookmakers have somehow managed to keep their margins up to the sort of levels not seen over here for about ten years. I'm not sure how, although there is plenty of money in Ireland at the moment, people want to bet, and the betting exchanges exert less of an influence on the racecourse market.

Racecourses here see bookmakers primarily as a source of income. They are a source of income, but the way to make money out of them is not to squeeze as much as possible out of the bookmakers themselves, but to recognise their value and importance in attracting racegoers. If racecourses allowed bookmakers in free, or allowed their staff in free, the ring would be stronger and more punters would go racing. Something should be done to protect bookmakers because the atmosphere they generate is priceless. It was a pity when technology put an end to the tic-tac man. Who hasn't, at some time in their life, waved their arms around in imitation of the tic-tac? There is no need for tic-tacs any more, and if racecourses don't cherish bookmakers, and allow them to wither on the vine, the day will come when they are an endangered species too. They may not be a racecourse manager's first choice for a dinner-party invitation, but if racecourses force bookmakers out of the game, in the end they'll regret it.

One of the problems bookmakers face is that punters are much more knowledgeable than they used to be. The educated punter of a few years ago would now be considered a mug punter, so there isn't as much 'mug' money around. There was a time when bookmakers could go 11-10 each of two and 6-4 the rag, and still take plenty of money, but not any more. Thanks partly to Pricewise, punters have been educated to pay more attention to value, and to shop around for the best price.

The fact is that nowadays there isn't much money in racecourse bookmaking at all. When you see a battered Volvo drive into a racecourse car park and four bookmakers tumble out, you know it isn't a thriving occupation. If you asked a captain of industry to examine the on-course business, he'd laugh his socks off because the profit margins are just not there and it's very labour intensive, with someone on the bookmaker's bag and someone on the computer as well as the bookmaker himself, and all of them being charged to get in, often to a half-deserted ring.

After the initial upheaval following the betting ring's reform in the late 1990s, the old faces eventually re-established themselves. I'd love to know what the average age of racecourse bookmakers is, but it certainly isn't low, and I can't imagine many 60-year-old bookmakers encouraging their 35-year-old sons to go into the business. At some courses the ring is so weak that it's not worth my while going. I won't go to Wolverhampton for a mid-week meeting, and I rarely go to Southwell because bookmakers there don't want to take a £200 bet on an 8-1 shot, because it will be the only £200 bet in the ring. If they do take it, the price collapses all the way along the line.

Maybe I should consider betting in Japan. The pool for the Prix de l'Arc de Triomphe must be the biggest of the year in France yet in 2006 Deep Impact's Japanese supporters were so fanatical, and so oblivious to the pari-mutuel odds, that he started at 2-1 on, even though bookmakers here returned an industry SP of 9-4 against. It was ridiculous. If that's the way Japanese punters normally bet, you could make a profit by flying to Tokyo and simply opposing all the big-race favourites.

These were some of the thoughts flitting through my troubled head in the early days of 2006 as I strode back, reasonably confident, into the betting ring, searching out the whites of those bookmakers' eyes.

CHAPTER NINE

CHELTENHAM ROLLERCOASTER

The last race has just finished, and I feel shell-shocked. What a day. I have never experienced anything like it. The opening day of the 2007 Cheltenham Festival. The ultimate rollercoaster.

There is nothing like the Cheltenham Festival. For purists, it is the pinnacle of the jumps season, full of history, heroes, memories, anticipation and excitement; the week when the best horses in Europe compete for one prestigious and valuable prize after another, in front of huge, noisy crowds. The setting is wonderful, with Cleeve Hill in the background, and the atmosphere electric. For me, it is a week when the betting market is tremendously strong and there are terrific opportunities for making my judgement pay. It's a huge betting week, the biggest of the year. Before it started I'd already had £10,000 on Detroit City at 5-1 for the Champion Hurdle and the same amount, at the same price, on Kauto Star for the Gold Cup, who I've since had another £3,000 on. This morning, Detroit City was 9-4 and Kauto Star 6-4, which gives me room for manoeuvre, if I want it.

I'm staying at the Dormy House Hotel, near Broadway, about fifteen miles from the racecourse. It's a lovely place. It should be, because it costs £250 a night during the Festival, and I paid for Monday night without being there. I intended to arrive in time for dinner but was tempted (not difficult) into a late night out in Cheltenham, and ended up sleeping on a sofa. I didn't even make it for their very nice breakfast. I went straight to the track.

I'd already studied the races until I was blue in the face and discovered that, in almost every race, the only horses I considered to be value were among the first five in the betting. If an outsider won, it would be a genuine outsider that I just couldn't find. Part of the reason, I think, is that the top trainers, with strength in depth in their yards, have now got the hang of the four-day Festival. The extra day – it was a three-day Festival until 2005 – dilutes the competitiveness of some races, which have a lot of runners but only a handful of real candidates.

They will all be running on faster ground than official going reports have suggested. At Cheltenham nowadays, the official going is more political than actual. Nine horses were killed during last year's Festival and they want to be seen to be racing on soft ground, which reduces the risk of fatalities. The meeting started with the ground officially soft, good to soft in places, but I was convinced it was quicker than that, and the times soon proved me right. After the third race, the official description changed to good to soft, soft in places. I think it was at least that to start with.

The upshot of all my theories is that I believe the favourites will do better than most people expect while the total SPs will be lower than the market expects. On the spreads, on the favourites' index, favourites earn 25 points for a win, 10 points for coming second, and 5 points for third place. In the SP market, the make-up is simply the cumulative total of all the winners' SPs. Mark and I have bought favourites at 185 points for the entire meeting, for £470 a point, and sold SPs at 285 points, for £440 a point. They are big bets, and the fairground ride started with a screaming plunge. Amaretto Rose, the hot favourite for the first race, the Supreme Novices' Hurdle, finished third. That wasn't disastrous, but the winner, Ebaziyan, was 40-1. At least it meant we'd quickly landed our ante-post bet that the longest-priced winner of the Festival would be at least 40-1, but that was a relatively small bet, because we couldn't get a lot on. In the Supreme Novices' I backed Granit Jack, Amaretto Rose and De Soto, all to win, and they finished second, third and fourth. I thought, is this a sign of things to come? I hoped not.

The next race was the Arkle Chase, over two miles. I'd spent the whole winter calling trainer Alan King a prat for thinking of running My Way De Solzen in the Arkle rather than the Ryanair Chase, which is over two miles five furlongs. At last year's Festival, My Way De Solzen won the three-mile World Hurdle. He's a horse I love, but I was convinced he'd be outpaced if he ran in the Arkle. Before Christmas, I wrote, 'My Way De Solzen will not win an Arkle Chase as long as night follows day, and I am amazed that his connections are still persisting with that pipedream.' Well, he did run in the Arkle, I backed his market rival, Fair Along, and My Way De Solzen wasn't outpaced. He must be a very special horse, because he won easily, with Fair Along, who started favourite, second.

Financially that wasn't great, but the Champion Hurdle was worse. It shows how obsessed we are with the Cheltenham Festival because just before this year's Champion Hurdle was run, Blue Square issued prices for next year's race! I think I'll wait a while.

For me, today's race revolved around Detroit City. If he

won, and I thought he would, I'd win £50,000. I was right in thinking that the old guard, Hardy Eustace and Brave Inca, would be beaten, although Brave Inca ran a cracking race to be second, but I didn't expect Sublimity to be the one to beat them, at 16-1. Detroit City went off at 6-4 and ran abysmally.

You know the old saying: just when you think things can't get worse . . .

The William Hill Trophy Handicap Chase is one of my favourite races of the Festival. Nowadays, trainers who have been cheating with their horses, to get their handicap marks down, find themselves ringing Phil Smith, the BHB's head of handicapping, to complain that their horse isn't rated high enough, which is why it has missed the cut for the William Hill Chase. The cheating horses aren't in it any more. It makes a pleasant change for Smith, who spends the rest of the year listening to trainers complaining that their horse is rated too high.

There are few things I like more than finding a 7-1 or 8-1 shot that I think represents good each-way value in a big-field handicap, and I'd found one in the William Hill. Among the 23 runners, the one for me was Juveigneur, the 7-1 co-favourite. Juveigneur always ran well at Cheltenham, and I liked his chances so much that I had £20,000 to £2,400 each-way on him. There was a time earlier in the season when I might have preferred someone other than Mick Fitzgerald to be on board, but as the months passed I had changed my mind. Fitzgerald seemed to have refocused, perhaps become more selective, now seemed certain to delay his retirement, and was riding really well. I was very happy to have him on my side.

After three miles, on the run-in, the race was between Juveigneur and Distant Thunder, one of the other co-favourites who I had also backed each-way. A few strides from the line, Juveigneur took the lead. Then, from way back, Joes Edge joined in. It was a desperately close three-way photo-finish. A lot of watchers thought Juveigneur had won. I knew he hadn't. The wait for the official announcement was almost unendurable, and when it came, it was agony: Joes Edge had beaten Juveigneur by a short-head, with Distant Thunder another short-head back in third place. To drive the stake right through my heart, and wallet, Joes Edge was 50-1.

When I plucked up the courage to watch a replay, I reached the conclusion that Fitzgerald, understandably, thought he just had to beat Distant Thunder to win, and rode Juveigneur perfectly to do that. Joes Edge came from so far back that, with the crowd roaring, I don't think Fitzgerald either saw or heard him. I am not knocking Fitzgerald, and even if he had known that Joes Edge was coming to challenge, Juveigneur may not have been able to find another inch. I don't suppose Fitzgerald was too pleased either.

Excluding Jackpot bets, a photo-finish has never cost me so much. The difference that short-head made was enormous. It plucked away the £20,000 Juveigneur's win would have made me and, on top of that horror, meant an extra 43 points on the SP market. At £440 a point, that translated into £18,920. Because Juveigneur's racecard number was the lowest of the co-favourites, he was treated as the favourite in the favourites' market. If he'd won, it would have been worth 25 points rather than 10 points. At £470 a point, that cost me another £7,050. So, altogether, that short-head cost me almost £46,000.

I'm good at taking reverses, but I'm finding it difficult to get this one out of my mind. I keep replaying the finish in my head. It wasn't £46,000 I actually had to pay, but it still felt as if the game was up. After only four of the meeting's 24 races, the SPs already totalled 109.5 points and the favourites only 25 points. My big ante-post bet on Detroit City had gone down and I felt as if I'd soon be looking on the internet for a false beard and cheap tickets to Paraguay. Either that or get back to the hotel and stab myself to death with a knife and fork. If that didn't work, I'd swallow the spoon. A silver one, probably.

Amazingly, the rollercoaster wasn't over. There were two races left, though it was difficult to focus on them. The first was the Sporting Index cross-country chase over almost four miles. It's a pretty silly race. Several of the big trainers ignore it, a lot of the runners are has-beens, and you can go off and have a cup of tea, come back and they are still going round and round in circles. When they finally finished, the 5-2 favourite, Heads Onthe Ground, was the winner, which suited me perfectly. It meant a winning favourite, 25 points, and only 2.5 to be added to the total winning SPs.

Every day I'm writing a piece for WBX, the World Bet Exchange, and recording tips for my telephone tipping line. For both, I named Gaspara as the bet of the meeting, in the Fred Winter Juvenile Novices' Handicap Hurdle, the last race of the opening day. Gaspara was a typical Pipe plot, although this year the Pipe is David rather than Martin. Three days ago, Gaspara romped home in the Imperial Cup at Sandown. If she won today, her connections would win a £75,000 bonus – the same bonus Martin Pipe landed with Olympian in 1993 and Blowing Wind in 1998. Gaspara only had a 4lb penalty for her Sandown success, and I thought she had a tremendous chance. Immediately after she won at Sandown I had £4,500 to £1,000 with Coral, and today I had £4,000 to £1,000 with Colin Webster. She won easily, at 9–2 joint favourite, and as her racecard number was lower than that of the other joint favourite, Pouvoir, she was treated as the favourite for the purposes of the favourites' index. Perfect. Another 25 points, and only 4.5 added to the SPs.

Somehow, we'd avoided imminent and complete disaster. Another 40–1 winner would have been almost too much to bear. It wasn't a great day, but it ended up a lot better than had seemed likely after the agony of Joes Edge. We were ahead of the game on the favourites' index and not hopelessly adrift on the SPs. In effect, we were about £6,400 down on those markets. Now I've got to get myself together for day two.

★

6.50 a.m., Wednesday, 14 March. I open the *Racing Post* and turn to Pricewise. I want to be with My Turn Now in the Ballymore Properties Novices' Hurdle, but on Betfair it is shorter than I expect, so I'm not surprised to see that Pricewise has gone for it under the headline 'Better ground can bring out the best in My Turn Now'. The early birds have already murdered the worm.

7.10. Breakfast at the Dormy House Hotel. Fruit, yogurt, then full English breakfast. You can't conquer Cheltenham on an empty stomach. I've already priced up the Ballymore and, having looked at the rest of the card, I don't feel as strongly about anything as I did about Detroit City and Gaspara yesterday. I'll be starting by concentrating on the day's two big handicaps, the Coral Cup and the Fulke Walwyn Kim Muir Chase. They are probably the day's least favourite races for most punters, but they are favourites with me. I'd love to find a horse I think is good value at 7-1 or 8-1, another Juveigneur, but without the photo-finish defeat. Yesterday's race still keeps popping into my head. I'd rather it didn't.

Early to Cheltenham, where the staff are already being given their briefings, and the media's day has started. It's another lovely, sunny day. In the press room, a handful of journalists have already arrived, and on the television sets Channel 4's Morning Line is about to begin. There's still the chance of a bit of peace and quiet. I spread out Whitley's sheets and put up Raceform Interactive on my laptop screen. Then I phone Mark to discuss the situation. We agree to stick with our bets on favourites and SPs. In fact, I'm tempted to go in again, and sell more SPs. I'm just not sure my nerves can take it. It's a white-knuckle bet.

By ten o'clock I've finished pricing up the first three races: the Ballymore, the Royal & SunAlliance Chase, and the Queen Mother Champion Chase. To my surprise, having looked for reasons to oppose Denman, the hot favourite for the SunAlliance, I've reached the conclusion that he could win by 25 lengths. The only other obvious front runner is Eurochancer, and I've got him in my tissue at 200-1. Denman travels so quickly that if he gets clear and into a rhythm, the horses chasing him will start to make mistakes. On Betfair he's 6-4, but I've put him in at 5-4 on. We've also backed Denman's rider, Ruby Walsh, to be top jockey at the meeting, at 7-4. So far no one has ridden more than one winner, and Walsh has had two seconds, which could be decisive in the end.

Denman is one favourite I expect to win, and Well Chief is another, in the Champion Chase. The evidence of his win at Newbury suggests that he's returned from injury as good as before, which was better than anything running against him today, and I don't think the bounce factor is a factor. He didn't have a hard race, and that was 32 days ago. I like Well Chief, and I'm against Newmill and Ashley Brook. The race fell apart when Newmill won it last year, with half the field not finishing, including Kauto Star, and I don't place much value on his recent hurdle defeat of Macs Joy and Harchibald, who are both on the missing list for Cheltenham. Newmill is generally 100-30, but I've priced him at 11-2 and will be looking to oppose him in match bets, along with Ashley Brook, who I feel might be going backwards this year.

11.40. I've finished pricing up the Coral Cup and Fulke Walwyn Kim Muir Chase.

In the Coral Cup, I'll be backing Burntoakboy, who is about 8-1. Somehow, Dr Richard Newland, his trainer, gets his horses to improve tremendously. Burntoakboy is a nine-year-old who joined Newland from Ireland last autumn and has got better with every race since. He still doesn't look as exposed as most of his rivals, and, whereas in his recent races he's been ridden by an amateur rider claiming 7lb, Burntoakboy is now ridden by Sam Jones, a good conditional jockey.

It's another race where I've ended up liking the front few in the market, including Oscatello, who Mark has backed at 20-1, and Mister Hight, and we'll be looking for match bets involving those horses against others. We'll also be backing the front five on my tissue to win because together they are 2-1 on with me, but about evens on Betfair. There are a lot of different ways of trying to make it pay.

At midday I wander down to Betfair's chalet in the tented village to join Steve Mellish, of Racing UK, and Matt Williams, of the *Racing Post*, on a panel of experts chaired by Sean Boyce of Attheraces. We all agree that Direct Flight is worth backing in the Fulke Walwyn Kim Muir Chase. Now with Charlie Egerton, Direct Flight has some encouraging form but hasn't run for almost a year. With Egerton training him, that is a possible plus, because there is nothing he likes better than to win a big race, first time out. It just goes to show how wrong you can be: Direct Flight is about to finish sixteenth of seventeen finishers.

Back to the press room, which is buzzing, and back on the phone to Mark. He is reining in my instinct to dive in and sell SPs again. I know there is a big potential downside. I've got a lot of horses in my tissues at 100-1, and if just one of them goes in we're in trouble. 'Who's going to drive the fast car to get us out of here?' I ask, only half-joking. Mark dissuades me, and has reduced our exposure in the SP market, which is just as well given that Massini's Maguire wins the opening Ballymore Hurdle at 20-1 with My Turn Now, whom we'd put £400 on at 10-1, finishing sixth.

I'm not going to dwell on it. I'm heading straight across to the pre-parade ring, to look at the runners for the SunAlliance Chase. There's multi-millionaire Sir Robert Ogden, aged 71, with his beautiful South American partner, aged about 31. How does that work, then? On a less exotic note, there's Barry 'The Judge' Court, busy demonstrating his unfailing ability to gain admission to places you wouldn't think would have him, in this case a place in the pre-parade ring a few yards from Princess Anne.

A professional paddock judge tells me that he's worried about the blotches on Denman's backside. Evidently they weren't there before Denman won impressively at Newbury last month. I still can't see them. To me, he looks magnificent, and, blotchy bottom or not, I'm planning to back him.

2.30 p.m. To the betting ring, where I have £2,000 on Denman at 5-4 with Colin Webster, then phone Mark, who has had £333 on Dom D'Orgeval at 9-1, and has bought the favourites' index again. I watch the race from near the winning post. Denman didn't win by 25 lengths, but he did win, easily, by ten lengths. It's a relief, because I hate backing short-priced favourites. It's also a boost for our spread bets.

While the unlikely partnership of Harry Findlay and Paul Barber, Denman's owners, are celebrating their hero's return to the winner's enclosure, I head straight back to the pre-parade ring to see how Well Chief is looking. His head looks fine, which is all you can see at the moment, because he's in a saddling box, surrounded by people. Once he emerges, an expert warns me that Well Chief is a bit warm between his legs. So am I, but I still feel fine. It doesn't put me off. I've already decided that if he wins, I'm going to make a donation towards jockey Timmy Murphy's wig.

Well Chief looks well, and so does Newmill, which tempers my enthusiasm for opposing him. Mark reminds me that, for some long-forgotten reason, Newmill is the second leg of a £50 each-way double we had just before Chicken Soup won at Chester last August. I think I'm safe in saying that no one else has had the same double.

Well Chief is the banker of the meeting for a lot of punters but he doesn't get beyond the second fence, which doesn't help the cause of our favourites' index bet. Even with Well Chief out of the running, Newmill can't manage better than fourth, and the only consolation is that the winner, Voy Por Ustedes, was 5-1, which helps on the SP front.

It's much better news in the Coral Cup, with Burntoakboy winning at 10-1. Good. In the Fulke Walwyn Kim Muir, we'll be cheering for Direct Flight, Cloudy Lane, and Yardbird. Cloudy Lane, the 15-2 favourite, does the decent thing. Fantastic. At last, we're cooking.

I know things are looking up because a man who has owed me four grand since the Ebor meeting at York last August suddenly hands me the lot, in cash. That has to be the shock result of the Festival. It's a good omen.

We've got nothing in the bumper, apart from five horses in the Placepot, each to a £4 unit stake. Only one of them is placed, the winner, Cork All Star, but it means we've got the Placepot four times, and it's a good one, paying £2,305.50 for £1. That's a return of £9,222. Cork All Star wasn't the favourite, but he was only 11-2.

We've had a mass of bets, and, when all the additions and subtractions have been done, I reckon I've won about £10,000 today. If I have a winning day tomorrow, then I can look forward to my £13,000 bet on Kauto Star knowing that it will have been a good Cheltenham, whatever happens in the Gold Cup. As I drive back to the Dormy House Hotel, I don't feel as tired as I did this morning. I've got an appetite for tomorrow.

★

When you are up you are up, and when you are down you are down, but when you are both up and down, you are at the Cheltenham Festival. Thursday, and one horse that could have made a big difference was Billyvoddan, in the Ryanair Chase. I'd backed him when he won a good handicap chase impressively at Ascot on his most recent outing, in December, and had always thought he'd make a very good chaser, even though his jumping was sometimes a bit clumsy. I wasn't surprised when his trainer, Henry Daly, decided to step him up in class, and this morning I backed Billyvoddan to win £50,000, at 33-1. Then I backed him on the spreads, buying £200 at 5 on a 50-25-10 index.

Four fences from home, Crozan fell, and hampered Billyvoddan, who was arguably unlucky to be beaten a neck and half a length by Taranis and Our Vic, with me screaming myself hoarse. We made a nice four-figure profit, but it was so close to being something a lot better. It was that sort of meeting from the start.

Mark was ducking in and out of the favourites' and SP index markets but, although we won about £3,000 on other bets in the World Hurdle, Black Jack Ketchum's early fall, when 2-1 favourite, wasn't good news. Nor were the exits of Nine De Sivola and Miko De Beauchene in the four-mile National Hunt Chase. We had backed the former at 16-1 and the latter at 12-1 and both of them went at the same fence, three from home, when both looked like being involved in the finish. I think Miko De Beauchene would have won. Instead, to rub salt into the wound, Butler's Cabin, who I didn't think would stay the trip, won at 33-1. Not good for our SP index bet. And the favourites? They didn't score a point between them, all afternoon. Every one was unplaced. Ow!

Thursday, in fact, has been a diabolical day. We aren't out, but we are certainly down, well down. I sincerely hope we are at the bottom of the rollercoaster ride, not only halfway down.

★

Gold Cup day, and Kauto Star isn't the valuable icing on the cake, as I'd hoped he would be by Friday morning. He is the cake. I've got £13,000 on him at almost 5-1, £2,000 of which is Mark's. After yesterday we need the Gold Cup favourite to win. Mercifully, gloriously, triumphantly, Kauto Star does, despite putting our hearts and other vital organs in our mouths with his trademark last-fence blunder.

That's over £50,000 in the plus column, plus 25 points for the favourites' index, and only 1.25 to be added to the SPs. When the final race, the County Hurdle, is over, the favourites, over the four days, have made up to 185 points – exactly what we bought them for. Despite all the upsets and long-priced winners, the SP total isn't disastrous. There were times, particularly after the first four races of the meeting, when I thought our bet could end up putting me out of the game altogether, but in the end it wasn't too bad. We sold SPs at 285 points, and the final make-up was 306 points, and we reduced the damage from that by trading in and out of the market.

Although it cost us money this year, I expect to be selling SPs again at Cheltenham next year. For the sake of my nerves, I may play day by day rather than over the whole meeting, and for a smaller stake, because there were times this week when it was difficult to think about anything else other than, what price is that horse, the one finishing well? It got in the way of enjoying it.

When everything – and there is an awful lot of it – has been added up, I've won about £50,000 this week, less my share of the £13,000 we put into another, oh so close, Jackpot attempt on the final day. There was a carryover of over £340,000, which built up to a pool of over £570,000. If only we had structured our perms slightly differently. I must stop saying 'if only'. In one line we had five winners and Whyso Mayo, beaten half a length in the Foxhunter Chase after bad jumping mistakes. In another line we had the 20-1 winner of the Foxhunter, Drombeag, but not Andreas, who won the Grand Annual Chase.

The Jackpot wasn't won, which led to a sting in the tail of my Cheltenham tale. With a carryover of £570,000, we had to go for it again at Uttoxeter on the Saturday. I hate Uttoxeter. I still remember the day, in 1988, when the first horse I owned, Dame Flora, was beaten there when odds-on. Saturday's experience didn't improve my opinion of the place, because when Mandatum fell at the last hurdle when looking certain to win the first race, our Jackpot bid was more or less over.

Unfortunately, as it turned out there was another carry-over to Carlisle the next day, when the pool reached over £1.8 million. The meeting should really have been abandoned, and with seventeen non-runners because of the desperate ground, there were only 53 runners to choose from. It was too many for us. Minster Abbi and Carapuce sank our boat, and most other people's. In the end, the Jackpot paid just over £100,000 to the holders of thirteen winning tickets. We weren't among them.

I hadn't got rid of all my Cheltenham winnings, but by Sunday evening I had lost almost half of them. I said it was a rollercoaster.

CHAPTER TEN

A CHILD'S PONY

Rishi Persad turned to me and said, 'Well, what a turn up, Dave. What do you think of that?'

If I'd told Racing UK's presenter exactly what I thought of it, it might have been my last television appearance, because I'd had the biggest single day-of-a-race bet of my life on a horse that had just been beaten a head, by a 100-1 shot.

It was Ebor day at York in August 2006. On big racedays, I've often done most of my betting by lunchtime, so I'm happy to appear on television. But smiling at the camera was a bit of a struggle at that particular moment. I'd fancied Glistening for the Ebor for quite a while, but he was regarded as a horse who needed good or faster ground to show his best form. Two days before the race, seventeen millimetres of rain fell at York and the going was officially changed to good to soft, with more rain forecast. On the morning of the race there was a strong wind blowing across the track, and I wasn't convinced that the going would necessarily ruin Glistening's chance. I had another look at his form. He'd been hampered in a good handicap at Epsom on Derby Day, been beaten a head by Young Mick in the Duke of Edinburgh Stakes at Royal Ascot after coming wide from a poor draw, then been beaten one and a half lengths, again by Young Mick, when third in another big handicap at Ascot in July, when the pace wasn't strong enough to suit him. At York, Glistening was 7lb better off with Young Mick, would appreciate the step up to one mile six furlongs, with an almost guaranteed decent pace, and he was trained by Luca Cumani, who had won the Ebor twice before. I was convinced that the Ebor was Glistening's race, and when I discovered that Jamie Spencer had been booked to ride him some time beforehand, I felt even more certain. Sometimes, in big handicaps, I have premonitions and convictions, and I had both about Glistening. I had £7,000 each-way on him.

It was a lot, but it wasn't all. I also had Glistening in a £100 each-way trixie (three doubles and a treble). My first selection, Topatoo, won the opening race at 14-1. That was another £3,000 going on to Glistening, plus the place money. So you can imagine that when Mudawin, the 100-1 shot, got up on the line to beat Glistening it was difficult to keep my professional broadcaster's hat firmly on my head rather than fling it away and replace it with my professional punter's hat, and stamp on that instead, while letting rip with a blood-curdling scream. After all, the photo-finish had cost me well over £60,000.

It got worse. In the final race at York the third horse in my trixie, Terentia, was also beaten a head, also at 13-2. Because it was an each-way trixie, and I had also backed the same horses in each-way singles, I still made what most punters would consider a cracking profit, but I couldn't help thinking that I'd been two heads away from winning a quarter of a million pounds. The fee from Racing UK didn't really make up for it.

★

Luca Cumani, Glistening's trainer, is one of several Flat trainers I respect, along with Saeed bin Suroor, Sir Mark Prescott, Richard Fahey, Mark Johnston, Michael Jarvis, and various others. Saeed bin Suroor trains for Godolphin, who have been terrific for punters over the years, regularly returning profits to level stakes. I used to think it was a great stable to follow, particularly their older horses, partly because you knew that Godolphin's runners were always trying. More recently, their horses seem to have been more heavily backed, so they don't represent as good value, and Godolphin has rather lost its focus. It was supposed to be a fairly small, elite stable, but it has become huge, more an enormous army than a select squad.

I admire Sir Mark Prescott, who is very good at placing his horses and planning their campaigns, but although he has had successes in pattern races, and certainly knows when he has a good horse, and how to train it, he is better known for running up sequences with less able horses. I am not knocking him, but it does get a bit boring watching staying horses who start their three-year-old season on a handicap mark of 50, gained by running over shorter trips as immature two-year-olds, beat up lesser horses at Musselburgh and Carlisle to win six races in a row. I'm not sure how admirable that is.

Nowadays, Prescott's horses tend to be short enough in the market, but you can sometimes get good value about Mark Johnston's horses. I wouldn't be frightened to back his stable's second string in a maiden race because you know it is there to win if it can, whereas with some other big stables you suspect that their second string is not there to win.

Richard Fahey is unusual because he is a talented trainer who was previously a jockey. Although there are plenty of former jockeys among Britain's trainers, I don't think many jockeys make good trainers. To me, that isn't surprising, because the two jobs are totally different. Just because a jockey rides work on a trainer's gallops, and then dashes off to a racecourse, doesn't equip him to be a successful trainer. He may be very good at race-riding but probably has no experience of actually buying or training horses, dealing with their physical problems, studying the programme book, entering horses for races, managing staff, or running a business, all of which you need to be a successful trainer.

My favourite trainer among the bigger names is undoubtedly Michael Jarvis. He was a private trainer for leading owner David Robinson in the late 1960s and early 1970s and is rock solid. He knows exactly what he is doing and never overplays his horses.

In contrast, there are trainers whose horses I don't like backing. Some trainers, although I am not saying they are bad trainers, are overrated. I think Barry Hills's reputation is based largely on the past. Nowadays, I think of him as a trainer who has a few short-priced winners at Doncaster and Chester, then largely disappears for the rest of the season.

When David Loder was training, I used to think that his reputation far exceeded his achievements. People regularly saw his name next to expensive maidens owned by Sheikh Mohammed and believed that they just had to go down to the start and come back again to stop being maidens, but a lot of them were beaten, and their average price was probably barely odds against.

To me, Paul Cole appears to be a social climber who looks a bit aristocratic and has mastered the art of getting hold of clients rather than the skills involved in being a master trainer. In my opinion, if some of the good horses he has trained had been trained by a better trainer, their record would have been better. Richard Hannon is another champagne trainer who has mastered the art of cultivating clients rather than horses. I've no idea why people have horses with him and his son because, apart from the Queen Mary Stakes, Fred Darling Stakes, and a few sales races, they win very few significant races. Anyone who can make money backing their horses is a genius.

You see some trainers standing in the owners and trainers bar at a racecourse, talking as if they are the elder statesmen of racing, with people eating out of their hands, despite the fact that they spend long spells on the *Racing Post*'s 'Cold Trainers' list and don't seem to know what they are doing.

It's probably impossible to do, but if someone like John Whitley, who is a statistician, could rank trainers on the basis of their performance, linked to the quality of the horses in their yards, perhaps based on the horses' purchase price, it would make fascinating reading. The trainers' table would certainly look very different. It would also be interesting to know how many horses enter each trainer's yard but never reach a racecourse. A lot.

Some yards, including Jeremy Noseda's and Brian Meehan's, are extremely 'leaky' when it comes to information, and the leakers are very bullish. I am not saying that Noseda and Meehan are bad trainers, but there seem to be an awful lot of punters in their yards who overrate the horses. As a result, their fancied horses rarely start at attractive prices. I know one man who paid a work rider at Noseda's £800 for tips, and was given only one winner. It's always worth asking yourself, if the work rider knows so much, why is he still shovelling shit at six o'clock every morning?

I have never been interested in information from stables, although I've had a lot of people offering it, as well as asking for it. When I started my weekly diary in the *Racing & Football Outlook*, at the beginning of 2000, the very first piece of advice I offered was that relying on inside information would send you skint. Phil Bull, the founder of Timeform, used to say that at the racecourse you should keep your eyes open and your ears closed, and I think that is very sound advice.

Information from some trainers is unlikely to be helpful because they are clueless about form. If they won as many races as they say they are going to, they'd be champion trainers. Philip Mitchell, for instance, is a lovely guy, but in my opinion he hasn't got a clue about form, and he's certainly not alone. Mitchell has been a terrific trainer of two horses: Attivo, whose big successes in the 1974 Triumph Hurdle, Chester Cup and Northumberland Plate came when trained by Philip's father, Cyril; and Running Stag, who won three Grade 2 races in America in 1999 and 2000. In September 1999 Running Stag finished fourth, beaten two lengths, in the Grade 1 Woodward Stakes at Belmont Park – top-class dirt form. Two months later he was 3-1 on in a small conditions stakes race at Lingfield, which he was entitled to be, because he officially had at least 23lb in hand of his rivals. Beforehand, Mitchell said he expected Running Stag to win easily, but after the horse had been beaten by Brilliant Red, Mitchell said he didn't think Running Stag had been fit enough.

It is common to hear trainers say, before a race, that their horse has just done a very good piece of work, then, after it has been beaten, say that they think it was short of work. It doesn't inspire confidence in the trainer, although Running Stag was ridden that day by Pat Eddery, who for me was a huge negative on all-weather tracks. After having spent a lot of winters abroad, Eddery started to ride on the all-weather tracks at a time when his career was on the wane. I don't think he liked it, and he wasn't good at it, but he still had a strong following among punters and his mounts often went off at short prices. They were always double the bookmakers' odds with me, and if Betfair had been around I'd have made a fortune laying them. I don't think I ever backed one of Eddery's all-weather mounts.

Trainers will sometimes ask me what chance I think their horse has got, because they are thinking of backing it and say they respect my judgement, but if I tell them that I think their horse has very little chance of winning, they still want to back it, because they have eyes only for their own horse, not for their opponents' horses. That explains why so many trainers are poor judges of whether or not their horse is likely to win. The better trainers don't know only about their own horses, they also know about the opposition – where the pace in a race is likely to come from, if anywhere, and how the race is likely to work out.

One of the reasons I like John Best as a trainer is that not only has he got a fair idea of what his own horses are capable of, he also looks at the opposition, asks people for their views, and tries to get a broader picture of each race.

Of course, it can be difficult to stick to your own judgement in the face of a trainer's opposing opinion. If his opinion is vindicated, it is difficult not to blame yourself for having foolishly ignored the view of the person seemingly best placed to know, the man who actually trains the horse concerned. Yet I know that, most of the time, that is what I should do – ignore what trainers say. After all, my professional survival depends on being better at interpreting form and expressing, in odds, each horse's chance of winning than other people. While many trainers have eyes only, or largely, for their own horses, I have eyes for every horse, so I will often know better than them.

When a friend who works for Brendan Powell asked me what chance I thought Warne's Way had of winning a novices' hurdle at Folkestone in February 2007, I told him that, on my reading of the form, there was a good chance of him being beaten and that he certainly wasn't an odds-on chance. Later, my friend rang to tell me that Powell thought I was talking nonsense. Even after sixteen years as a professional punter I am still capable of falling into the same traps as failed punters, and instead of sticking to my guns, I backed down, allowed myself to be influenced, and bought the favourites' index for £100 just before Warne's Way ran, starting at 10-11. Then I watched him finish fifth, and lost about £2,500. It was the act of an idiot, but anyone who says they are totally on the ball the whole time and never slips up is lying. Everyone allows themselves to be influenced at least sometimes by what other people say, but you have to try to trip up less often. If the Warne's Way experience means that

I am less likely to repeat it, then the £2,500 will have been well spent.

Another thing I like about John Best is that he runs his horses quite a lot, yet still maintains a good strike rate. Generally, I like trainers who run their horses regularly because in the case of moderate handicappers, which is what most horses are, you have to run them for handicapping reasons. A horse may be capable of winning off a mark of 58 but not off a mark of 65. Typically, the horse may enjoy a period of good form for two six-week periods each year, during which, hopefully after a couple of wins, his handicap rating will be up to 65. The only way to get the horse's rating down to a winning level again is to run it. I don't mean running it not to win, I just mean running it.

★

The rules say that jockeys mustn't bet, but over the years a lot of them have wanted me to put money on for them, in return for information, the information being that they want to back a particular horse. They don't want to part with their own money, though. A jockey will ask me to put £100 on a horse for him and you sit there, waiting for the £100 to be produced, but it doesn't appear. I'd love to bet in the way they want to, without having to pay.

Although the best jockeys tend to be on the best horses, I still think that the public and the bookmakers underestimate the value of a good jockey. At the moment, the top Flat jockey in my book is Ryan Moore, who I think is terrific. Jamie Spencer is good but can be a bit of a prima donna, Frankie Dettori is very Italian – brilliant, then awful.

The awful includes his ride on Establishment in the 2002 Ascot Stakes, when Dettori was beaten a head after sitting too far off the pace. I couldn't help noticing, because it was my biggest bet of the year. At least I'd backed it each-way, although when a horse you've backed is an unlucky loser, it doesn't make you feel any better when someone inevitably says, 'You backed it each-way, though, didn't you?'

John Egan and Oscar Urbina have both been riding very well recently, and I think Chris Catlin is underrated. George Baker is good, as are Neil Callan and Paul Hanagan. Martin Dwyer is solid, Seb Sanders is strong but often has the advantage of being on a Prescott hotpot, while Eddie Ahern and Darryll Holland both have a habit of riding themselves into trouble. Holland is very strong but not, I think, good tactically, which has also sometimes been a weakness with Robert Winston. At one time, Holland seemed to be cursed when I backed his mounts, prompting me to call for the introduction of a special 'palpable error' rule, under which any bet placed by me on a horse ridden by Holland was deemed to be void.

One jockey who certainly isn't tactically weak is Philip Robinson. One day at Newmarket in November 2003 he was the only jockey to come up the stands rails, on Babodana, despite the fact that most of the previous day's winners had done so. Robinson made all the running and won at 25-1. One of my favourite in-running bets is if there is a fancied horse, trained by Michael Jarvis and ridden by Robinson, that is in front after a furlong. In those circumstances, the partnership has a terrific strike rate. Between them they have masses of experience, they both know what they're doing and, if they are confident enough to go out and try to make all on a horse whose chances they clearly fancy, it almost certainly deserves to be odds-on in-running.

One of the jockeys who chose not to come up the stands rails at Newmarket when Babodana won, despite being drawn 1, was Richard Hughes. One of my jockey angles is to oppose Hughes in match bets because he strikes me as a jockey who doesn't believe in riding out hard once his chance of winning the race has gone.

Richard Hills, who has one of the smallest fan clubs in racing, lost another member after the ride he gave Amoras at Salisbury in June 2002. Hills rides well from the front but otherwise tends to go as wide around the outside as a belt on the world's biggest darts player.

There are some jockeys whose mounts I just won't back, a list to which Michael Tebbutt's name was added after the ride he gave Zonergem at Goodwood in July 2002. Tebbutt reported that Zonergem, who had a reputation for being quirky, hit his head on the starting stall and 'ran like a drunk', but he wasn't running like a drunk when he flew down the outside to finish third, with Tebbutt appearing to drop his hands near the finish. The stewards held an inquiry, 'noted' Tebbutt's explanation, and took no further action. The action I took was to make sure there wasn't a punter in Bognor Regis who hadn't heard the Zonergem story at least twice before closing time.

Some people, particularly jockeys, think you have no right to criticise them if you haven't been a jockey yourself, which is absolute nonsense. It is easier for an observer to see what is going to happen during a race than it is for a jockey riding in it, and it can be a painful experience. Watching a jockey make a decision that puts him in a position from where, perhaps because of the pace, you know he won't be able to win, or the gap he needs won't come, is agony. Sometimes you wonder if a poor decision was deliberate, and in the *Racing & Football Outlook* I have sometimes been outspoken about poor rides. If someone rides a shocker, I am entitled to say so. There is a lot of preciousness about jockeys, not all of whom are particularly good race-riders.

Once, when I approached the Lingfield stewards about a suspect ride, the stipendiary steward virtually dismissed my complaint on the grounds that I was talking through my pocket. Of course I was talking through my pocket, but that doesn't prevent me looking at a race objectively. If I'm financially involved, I will be looking particularly closely. Either through incompetence or villainy, I had just had my pocket picked by a jockey, and it was the stewards' job to decide which.

I think Britain's handicap system is a pretty good one, but it does mean that a horse's connections will be keen for their horse to have a favourable handicap mark, and some people will cross the line between gamesmanship and crookery in order to get one. It is a game of cops and robbers, but I think there should be better-qualified policemen on the beat, and villains should be locked up more often. Stewards should use their powers more often than they do at the moment to refuse to take account of a particular race when determining a horse's handicap mark.

Stewarding has certainly become more professional, but a multi-million-pound industry which is trying to sell itself around the world should not be so dependent on volunteers who happen to have plenty of spare time and can afford to do the job for nothing. There should be more paid stewards, but the resources probably aren't there to offer salaries high enough to attract suitably qualified applicants.

I certainly think jump racing is straighter than Flat racing. One of the things that helped get my professional punting career going, about a year after I started, was spotting that Tony McCoy, who was then a conditional jockey, was something special. In 1994 and 1995, when he was still claiming an allowance, I thought he was already 7lb better than most other jockeys. As far as I was concerned, it was Christmas time.

McCoys don't come along very often but if you can spot a new talent early, it can be worth a lot of money. I was a fan of Ryan Moore's from early in his career, and, over jumps, Robert Thornton was very good value for his claim. In 1996, as an amateur, he won twice on a horse I part-owned called Rosie-B, first at Newton Abbot, at 11-2, when Thornton claimed 7lb, and then at Taunton, when he claimed 5lb. I wasn't so pleased with him at the 2007 Cheltenham Festival, however, when I backed Ruby Walsh to be the leading jockey, and Thornton pipped him for the title.

★

Rosie-B, like most of the horses I have owned or part-owned, was good enough to win races, but not good enough to win good races. Almost without exception, the horses I have bought have been cheap horses. They have done well, at their own modest level. People assume that I have the pick of the horses John Best and I buy, and that I keep the best ones, but it is actually the other way round. I keep the ones we haven't been able to sell, or the parts of them that are unsold.

Until Rising Cross came along, the best horse I owned was probably a jumper called Mercato. He was already at John's yard when I bought him for next to nothing, and he soon set what may well be a record. At the end of 2002, when he was a six-year-old, we sent Mercato novice chasing, choosing good-class races with small fields, the sort of fields that wouldn't be allowed today. Mercato started at Ascot, in a six-runner race, and finished last of the four finishers. I collected £1,650. He then finished third of five at Cheltenham – another £2,310. After eight novice chases, Mercato had beaten only four finishers, but he'd picked up £14,800 in prize money.

Although still a maiden over fences, Mercato had ability. He was well suited by the conditions of the military races run at Sandown Park each year, and in February 2004 I leased him for the day to Colonel R. Symonds, to run in the Royal Artillery Gold Cup. We arranged for Captain Alex Michael, who had won the race in 1999 on Carlisle Bandito's, to ride. It was like coming into contact with another world. Michael was a nice man and came to the yard to ride Mercato, but it was very Biggles and 'chocks away, chaps'. At Sandown, his mother brought some chocolate cake for us. That was very nice, too.

Mercato finished a creditable second to Gunner Welburn, and a couple of weeks later was third to Grey Abbey and Royal Auclair, two top-class chasers, at Doncaster. A week after that it was back to Sandown for the Alvis Grand Military Gold Cup. At last, this time ridden by Captain Rupert Sturgis, Mercato finally broke his chasing duck and won by fifteen lengths, at 9-2. I was on cloud nine.

I was also on champagne. That is my excuse for succumbing to the urgings of the press photographers and mounting the podium to join the winning jockey and receive the winning owner's trophy. I'd forgotten that Mercato had been leased for the day. Too late, I suddenly realised that I shouldn't be the one gleefully clutching the trophy, while the cameras clicked, and the owners for the day scowled at me from nearby. When I stepped down, the temporary owner's wife stepped up and said, 'I rather thought that my husband and I might be collecting the trophy.' It wasn't the proudest moment of my life, nor the most gracious.

That autumn, Best and I were looking for yearlings again, helped by Anthony Bromley and David Minton of the Highflyer Bloodstock agency. They would ring John from the sales each morning to tell him about horses they had seen which they thought might interest us. One day in September 2004 we received a call from Minton, who was at Tattersalls Ireland yearling sales. He'd found a likely candidate in the form of a filly by Cape Cross, called Rising Cross, who had fetched 10,500 guineas as a foal. She was a bit small, said Minton, but looked as if she might go a bit. John rang me and I looked at her pedigree. Rising Cross's dam, Woodrising, had won three claiming races on the Flat, and three over hurdles. Her final triumph had been in a selling hurdle at Hexham in 1998, when she was bought in for 3,200 guineas. Still, Cape Cross was a better sire than most of our previous purchases boasted, and there was enough encouragement in the pedigree for us to give Minton the go-ahead. He bought Rising Cross for 20,000 euros, which was then the equivalent of about 13,000 guineas.

I was at John's yard when the filly arrived in a horsebox from Ireland. When she walked down the ramp, I burst out laughing. That year, the average sale price of Cape Cross yearling fillies in Britain and Ireland was over 41,000 guineas. It was immediately obvious why we had been able to buy this one for less than a third of that. She was ridiculously small. Minton must either have been drunk when he bid for her, or viewed her while on his knees. Or he was trying to stitch us up. I said to John, 'She's not a racehorse.'

I rang Minton and told him, 'Don't do that to us. We've bought enough horses through you now. There's no need to treat us like that.'

'She'll be OK,' he said. 'Don't worry. She'll be OK.'

I didn't believe him. He'd certainly bought something with my money, but whatever it was, it wasn't a racehorse. A child's gymkhana pony, perhaps, if the child was a small one.

Best's horses did well that winter and, partly as a result, they were selling well. I'd take my two girls to the yard on

Sunday mornings and there'd often be owners and potential owners there, and we'd sometimes sell part of a horse. But I couldn't think of any part of Rising Cross that anyone was likely to want to buy. I just reconciled myself to the fact that I was stuck with her. If the worst came to the worst, I could eat her. A couple of family dinners would be enough to see her off.

One day, three men turned up who had never owned a horse before but wanted to. They hadn't got a lot of money but were real enthusiasts. With trepidation, we led out Rising Cross, closed our eyes, and waited for their reaction. They didn't laugh, and a couple of days later came back to say that they wanted to buy her but could only afford half of her. I did my best to sell them the other half, offering deferred payment, but they wouldn't budge, so I was stuck with half of Rising Cross. We set up the Heading for the Rocks Partnership, which said it all.

On her first outing, at Windsor in April 2005, Rising Cross did better than we expected, finishing fifth of fifteen. She then finished fourth at Folkestone and fifth, at 25-1, in the listed five-furlong Hilary Needler Trophy at Beverley. On 21 June, Rising Cross returned to Beverley, this time over seven and a half furlongs in a weaker, maiden auction fillies' race, and won. She had already exceeded my expectations, but promptly won again, a nursery at Newmarket worth over £10,000 to the winner, off a rating of 78.

It was already clear, although it took me a long time to acknowledge it, that despite her diminutive stature, Rising Cross was a useful racehorse. After finishing fourth in a listed race at Sandown to Confidential Lady, who later won the Group 1 Prix de Diane at Chantilly, Rising Cross won a conditions race at Newmarket, finished fourth in two Group 3 races, and was then runner-up to Nannina in the Group 3 Prestige Stakes at Goodwood, at 14-1. She was a tough little lady, and finished the season, her eleventh race, with a sixth place in the Group 2 May Hill Stakes at Doncaster.

Jamie Spencer, who had partnered Rising Cross five times, said that it was like riding a snake, but he was still complimentary about her. Spencer said she was one of the toughest horses he had ever ridden. Even so, that autumn I was even more desperate to sell my half than I had been in the spring, for two reasons. First, I took the view that she couldn't possibly train on. She was small, didn't have scope, had had a busy season, and would soon be overtaken by an army of bigger, slower-maturing fillies. Second, I needed the money, because the final few months of 2005, as I've already described, were disastrous from a betting point of view.

To my relief, it was agreed that we would send Rising Cross to Tattersalls October Sales. We asked three bloodstock agents for advice on the reserve we should place on her, and all three suggested over 100,000 guineas. To be certain of a sale, I persuaded my partners to put her in with a reserve of 80,000 guineas. The bidding stopped at 77,000 guineas, and back she came to Best's yard, still owned by the Heading for the Rocks Partnership. I imagined people had taken one look at her (if they could see her) and thought the same as me, that she couldn't possibly train on.

Before the Flat season started, Best suggested that we

enter the stable star for the Oaks, at an initial cost of £800, plus a further £2,600 later on. I flatly refused, insisting that it was a waste of money. After three unsuccessful runs in listed races at Lingfield and Kempton in the spring, my opinion seemed, sadly, to have been vindicated. Rising Cross's small bubble had apparently burst, but in the Masaka Stakes at Kempton she suffered a troubled run and on 6 May she dead-heated to win the Lupe Stakes at Goodwood. I immediately became a belated convert. With the Oaks field falling apart, I was suddenly as keen to pay £20,000 to supplement her for Epsom as I had been opposed to paying £800 two months earlier.

Understandably, Best insisted that it be me who phoned the other members of the partnership to suggest that they hand over £10,000. There was prize money down to sixth place and the argument for running was that if she came fifth, it would only have cost us about £8,000; if she did better than that, we'd be in pocket. I thought that was a good bet, but I was still expecting resistance. Luckily, my partners were on a high after the Lupe and immediately said yes.

It was a first runner in a Classic for John Best, a first ride in one for George Baker, and a first for me, too. And Oaks day 2006 turned out to be the most exciting racing day of my life. Virtually no one thought we had a chance. After commenting that Rising Cross was 'not a very big filly' and that the Lupe was not a very good trial for the Oaks, Epsom's racecard dismissed Rising Cross with the verdict, 'her odds of around 40-1 do not appeal as being especially generous'. I didn't agree. I thought she was underrated and overpriced.

One of my partners had backed her at 100-1, and I backed her, each-way, at 66-1, as well as buying her on the spread indexes, and selling her finishing position at 6.5 in a field of ten. We knew one thing about her for certain: she had tremendous courage and guts, and she didn't like being beaten. While most horses disappoint you and you go home after most races feeling deflated, Rising Cross was a horse who never let you down. If you could find a way of putting her courage into horses a size and a half bigger, it would be a tremendous winning formula.

In the parade ring, Rising Cross and George Baker looked ridiculous – the tallest jockey on the smallest horse – but the race went like clockwork. Baker's instructions were to sit mid-division, pick the leaders off if he could, and finish in the best position possible. That is what happened. As they came down the hill, George switched Rising Cross to the outside, and just for a moment I thought she might win. I could see that she was going to beat all the horses in front of her, but then, just as my confidence was rising, Kieren Fallon shot past on Alexandrova, the Aidan O'Brien-trained favourite, and it was all over. As Alexandrova cut in front of Rising Cross, our filly stumbled and almost unseated Baker, but he picked her up and she kept on bravely to be second, at 33-1.

I was screaming her home, then flew down the stairs to greet her, with my partners leaping up and down. God knows what it must be like to win a Classic, because it was exhilarating finishing second. I'd never had a really good horse before. People still come up to me and congratulate me, and I still get excited thinking about it. David Minton hadn't paid us much attention in the parade ring before the race, but he paid us a lot of attention afterwards. It was a day of days, and supplementing Rising Cross for £20,000 had proved well worthwhile. The prize for finishing second was almost £95,000.

Within a couple of weeks, Gary Tanaka offered us £325,000 for Rising Cross. When I asked my partners if they wanted to accept the offer, they said yes, which was my preference too. Not bad for a small horse that cost less than £14,000. Tanaka's strategy was to buy established performers and, unless they seemed likely to thrive in the USA, leave them with the trainers who had been successful with them. So Rising Cross remained with Best and was supplemented for the Irish Oaks, finishing third to Alexandrova, then winning the Group 2 Park Hill Stakes at York, at 16-1, winning me £10,000 in bets.

Rising Cross is an amazing horse, and she is still in training with Best. He says she has grown a bit, but she's still under fifteen hands.

CHAPTER ELEVEN

THE TIME OF MY LIFE

Good news for bookmaker Barry Dennis. The great gambling gods in the sky punished me for that October day at Windsor in 2000 when I took £5,000 off Dennis by backing Square Dancer and Chorus, both at 25-1. Since then, Windsor has never failed to welcome me with the warm embrace of a crematorium furnace. For some reason, but not a good one, I keep stepping back into the coffin.

On 10 April 2006, I extended a string of losing bets at Windsor by having £666 on Summer's Eve, in running, at odds of 1.15. She was caught by The Last Drop. Half an hour later, I backed Greenwood each-way at 20-1 in a sixteen-runner handicap. Crimson King was taken out, and Greenwood finished – you've guessed it – fourth. Misfortune is the gambler's faithful companion, and he/she certainly never misses a meeting at Windsor. There, disaster is de rigueur. At the end of that afternoon, I vowed never to go again. A few weeks later, I found myself writing, 'After all these years, I have still not learnt that Windsor on a Monday night is possibly the most financially injurious form of racing known to man.' Foolishly, I had broken my vow and presented myself at the crematorium for another roasting, which was duly supplied. If I am seen betting there again, please ask a security guard to escort me off the premises, for my own safety.

Luckily, not everywhere is Windsor on a Monday night, and 2006 was a much better year for me than 2005. It needed to be. My decision at the end of 2005 to change strategy worked. I abandoned the living-room sofa and the temptations of Trisha and The Jeremy Kyle Show and returned to the racecourse, my natural betting home. I largely gave up winter all-weather racing in favour of the jumps. I concentrated on the bigger races and bigger race meetings, and had bigger bets, although after the disasters of late 2005 it took me a while to summon up the courage to increase the size of my bets. By the standards of most professional punters, however, they were already big. And I focused more on the big pool bets, the Jackpot and Scoop6, because that is where I believe many of the best-value bets now lie.

Betfair was a brilliant idea, brilliantly executed, but betting on betting exchanges increasingly reminds me of trading on currency markets. You are betting against some of the best betting brains in the world. You can't see the people you are betting against, some of whom have information you don't have. As a result, the market on Betfair now provides a more accurate picture of the true winning chance of each horse than ever before. You have a near-perfect market in which I can still make a profit, but I have to turn over a lot of money to do so because the margins are small. I think it will end up as a market in which no one will win a lot of money, apart from Betfair itself, from its commission charges.

On the face of it, Tote Jackpot and Scoop6 bets do not seem particularly attractive because there is a 29 per cent deduction from Jackpot pools and a 30 per cent deduction from Scoop6 pools. That is a lot higher than the takeout rates in, for instance, New York, where the takeout from Pick 6 pools is only 15 per cent on days when there is no carryover and 25 per cent when there is. I think it was Andy Beyer, the inventor of Beyer speed ratings and the *Washington Post*'s racing correspondent, who first pointed out that the higher takeout rates on exotic bets like the Pick 6 conceal the fact that these bets offer better value than win bets, on which the takeout in New York is now 15 per cent, and in Britain 13.5 per cent. That is because the Jackpot and Pick 6 are effectively six bets, with a single deduction. The takeout from the Jackpot pool is roughly 5 per cent per race, and when there is a carryover, which is the only situation in which Mark and I will get involved, the takeout rate is diluted.

Another attraction is that, instead of betting against the big brains on Betfair, many of whom rarely, if ever, do the Jackpot or Scoop6, I can bet against an army of less sophisticated punters, which should give me an edge. Jackpot punters have to be less well informed, otherwise no one would have a Jackpot bet when there is nothing in the pool and the guaranteed minimum pool is only £10,000. Since the Jackpot seems to be getting more popular, and building up more quickly, I think the Tote should increase the guaranteed minimum to £25,000.

Inevitably, you get five winners more often than six, and I know all about the frustration of repeatedly hitting the crossbar, but I am convinced that exotic pool bets are worth focusing on, and I think Mark and I play them well. My tissues combined with Mark's skill in constructing permutations based on them is a good combination.

In 2007, chasing the post-Cheltenham Festival Jackpot was not a happy experience, but in 2006, chasing the post-Cheltenham Scoop6 was a very happy one. Saturday, 18 March was Winter Derby day at Lingfield and Midlands

Grand National day at Uttoxeter, a course I approached with the usual trepidation. The big race at Uttoxeter was won by the favourite, G V A Ireland, but the totescoop6 Handicap Hurdle was won by a 14-1 shot, Heir To Be, and the Winter Derby by Sri Diamond, at 8-1. Those results knocked most players out of the pool, and by the time the final leg arrived, Mark and I had the sole remaining ticket. When Something romped home at Lingfield, we won £96,645.

In July, after a flurry of successes, including a decent win on Fairmile in the John Smith's Cup at York, I went to Monte Carlo for a week of luxury. A month later, at York's Ebor meeting, Mark and I had 2.5 of the seven winning Jackpot tickets, each paying £18,281. We won the Jackpot again at Lingfield on 5 October. Unfortunately, five of the six winners were favourites and the sixth was second favourite, so we were not alone. There were 138 winning tickets in the pay-out queue, each claiming £1,452, which was less than half what we had staked. Less than three weeks later, on Champion Stakes day at Newmarket, we shared in a near £1 million Scoop6, with our two winning tickets worth over £31,000, and then won a modest share of the following week's £558,000 bonus.

Despite the blip after the Cheltenham Festival, we have had more Jackpot successes this year, 2007. On 12 January, at Huntingdon, we won £16,500; at Taunton on 8 February we won over £4,000; and at Wincanton on 8 March over £7,000. Not huge, but worth having.

It wasn't all plain sailing. At Sedgefield on 20 February, the Jackpot reached over £1 million, and we put about

£17,000 into the pot, more than we have ever staked on a Jackpot before. I arrived at the racecourse late, but not too late to be told that Wise Owl had been beaten at 2-1 on in the first. At least I was spared the agony of watching it. That killed about 15,000 of our lines, and the remaining 2,000 disappeared when Neptune Joly won the second. Losing £17,000 in 40 minutes isn't a great feeling and makes it seem an awfully long way back to Tunbridge Wells.

Of course, what you shouldn't do in that situation is succumb to the temptation to chase – a thoroughly tried and tested way of making things worse. I wouldn't say I was guilty of chasing at Sedgefield, because my bets on the last four races involved backing horses I thought were tremendous value, all of them favourites, but there was certainly an element of the professional smash-out about it. By the time Top Cloud, Nevada Red, Waking Ned and Never So Blue had won, I had more than halved our losses. It wasn't a good day, but it was a lot better than had seemed likely at 2.30 p.m.

Once you have command of the form, the key to successful betting on horseracing is being able to identify situations when the margins are against you, and when they are in your favour, and learning how to exploit potentially favourable situations. I think that the Jackpot and Scoop6 provide good opportunities, and spread betting will always be part of my operation, as long as I can get the bets on. Otherwise, my expectations for day-to-day betting have fallen. I still expect to grind out a profit, but, because of the changed nature of the market and the margins, I don't expect to make a fortune, day to day.

In 1994, after Eddie Fremantle had shown me how to construct a tissue, and what to do with it, we were sometimes the only racecourse punters who knew that a particular horse showing on one or more bookmakers' boards at 16-1 should have been 8-1. I used to wear a pair of shoes out every month walking up and down the bookmakers' lines looking for a price that was out of line, and for a bookmaker who set his own prices, based on his own opinions. Now, Betfair lets everyone know what price each horse should be and bookmakers don't set their own prices any more. The last career you would want to pursue now is that of a horserace odds-compiler. Who needs them, when there is Betfair?

As for a career as a professional punter, it is important to bear in mind that it is not just a matter of making your betting pay, although that is hard enough. You have to have the right personality and temperament, too, because it is an alternative lifestyle, and brings its own pressures and problems. I don't stand there peering through my binoculars, as cool as the proverbial cucumber, holding all the aces and knowing that I do. I am the Cincinnati Kid, at the 'chancer' end of the spectrum rather than at the unflappable, Edward G. Robinson end. Somehow, you have to survive the slings and arrows of outrageous misfortune that inevitably come flying in your direction, without shooting yourself in the foot, and it isn't easy.

Although, as I said, I think I am good at dealing with reverses, that only means good in comparison with most other punters. I am still capable of being 200 miles from home, £2,000 worse off than when I set off, and fed up. I can still get home, not pay my partner as much attention as I should – because I want to get straight down to studying the next day's card, to put things right – and then have a row. When things are going badly – sometimes, it seems, in every part of your life – you say things you don't really mean, usually to someone close to you. I know I sometimes have.

I think that a life in which gambling plays such a big part has slightly impaired my ability to form true partnerships with people. A counsellor I have been seeing is concerned that my main relationship is with gambling and that other relationships, in reality, are secondary. Sadly, I think there is some truth in her suggestion, but I believe there is still room for stable relationships to flourish. I certainly hope so.

Professional gambling has given me a great life, and it's given my children and Lotte a lovely life and a lovely home, but I do sometimes look at my brother, who has a very different character, and wonder which of us is better off. My brother is not ambitious and is never distant with people in the way I know I can sometimes be. He is very relaxed and always smiling – God knows why, because he is a policeman in Newcastle – and he thinks he has a great life, too. He certainly isn't forever thinking about the next day's racing, or wondering how he is going to make the £20,000 a month I need to make.

Lotte and I are separated. She and our children live in the lovely big house we had built four years ago in Sevenoaks, while I am living in a rented flat in Tunbridge Wells. My rent is almost £2,000 a month, and I give Lotte over £10,000 a month. I don't begrudge it, but it's hard getting it. There are school fees for the children, and for the horses. Of course, I could sell the horses, but I want to carry on living the dream, and I will carry on living it as long as I can. The need to make a lot of money certainly keeps me on my toes.

By the end of March this year, 2007, I had already made a profit of over £70,000, and I am hopeful that it will be my best year yet. Mark and I are winning Jackpots and getting close to having a big one for ourselves. Recently, we won the Jackpot yet again. At Nottingham, on 17 April, when the pool contained £587,827, we held two of the 18.5 winning tickets, each worth £22,560. Eight days later, at Epsom, with £115,526 in the pool, we had one of just three winning tickets, worth over £27,000. I think it's reasonable to believe that around the corner there is a big Jackpot with our name on it – perhaps a £400,000 Jackpot or a £1 million Scoop6 – as long as we are still in the game, and still able to pay the stake. That is my pension plan.

I doubt if I am financially better off now than I was before I became a professional punter, but every day I am doing what I want to do. It is a life that has its difficulties, financial and otherwise, but I love doing it, and I want to carry on doing it. I get up every morning and feel glad that I will be going racing. In the winter, when racing starts early, and I catch an earlier train, it is full of businessmen from the stockbroker belt I live in, and I give thanks that I am not one of the commuters standing for the daily grind into London. Things would have to get bad for me to consider doing that.

What I may do in years to come is get more involved in

the bloodstock market. At the moment I am clearing the decks and only have two horses in training, King After and Bertie Southstreet, and a half-share in Sharp Stanley. John Best and I have learnt how to campaign horses with a view to selling them, and when I get that big Jackpot up I will be stepping into the market again, but at a higher level. We have done well with cheap horses, but I think that with polytrack being laid across America there will be more interest than before in horses who have won maiden races at Lingfield, and all-weather maiden races generally will become more competitive. I may do something on my own, or with a handful of people who are in a financial position to invest in decent yearlings. I haven't got a big enough pot at the moment, but I will get there.

As for the decision I took fourteen years ago, to become a professional punter, I have absolutely no regrets. I have had the time of my life. It's been quite a chunk of my life, and I hope there is still a big chunk more.

INDEX

INDEX